# UNIX Tool Building

# UNIX Tool Building

## Kenneth Ingham

Computer & Information Resources & Technology (CIRT)

University of New Mexico

Albuquerque, New Mexico

**Academic Press, Inc.**

Harcourt Brace Jovanovich, Publishers

San Diego   New York   Boston   London

Sydney   Tokyo   Toronto

This book is printed on acid-free paper. ∞

Academic Press, Inc.
San Diego, California 92101

United Kingdom Edition published by
Academic Press Limited
24–28 Oval Road, London NW1 7DX

Library of Congress Cataloging-in-Publication Data

Ingham, Kenneth, date
    Unix tool building / Kenneth Ingham.
       p.  cm.
    Includes bibliographical references.
    ISBN  0-12-370830-3  (alk. paper)
    1. UNIX (Computer operating system)   I. Title.
QA76.76.063I54   1990
005.4'3--dc20                                              90-527
                                                            CIP

Printed in the United States of America
90  91  92  93     9  8  7  6  5  4  3  2  1

To my parents

# Contents

**C H A P T E R   1**

**C H A P T E R   2**

**C H A P T E R   3**

## CHAPTER 4

**Parsing the Control File** ...................................... 41

## CHAPTER 5

**Compiling and Maintaining the Code** .......................... 57

## CHAPTER 9

## CHAPTER 10

## APPENDIX A

# Preface

With UNIX becoming more widespread, more people are using it to write large programs. However, much of the knowledge of how to use the tools provided with UNIX to write new tools exists in people's heads, transferred from person to person or else learned through experimentation and many frustrating days poring over the manual and wondering what the author *really* meant.

The goal of this book is to explain some of these tools in more detail as well as to introduce the reader to some of the concepts of tool building. Anyone can write programs. With a little forethought, these programs could be more general and have uses beyond just solving the one problem they were designed to solve. When thought is given to debugging before a program is written, debugging aids can be built into the program to reduce the debugging time.

Many small examples highlight specific ideas. However, as the book progresses, a large program is built to illustrate the concepts presented, tying the use of tools together and providing a unifying example. This example program makes *UNIX Tool Building* unique among books discussing programming and UNIX.

The examples used in this book worked on Ultrix 3.1, a version of UNIX based on Berkeley 4.3BSD. Output from sample commands will vary between systems.

Many people helped me write this book. Most notable were Keith Nislow who helped improve my writing skills and gave numerous comments on the style. Pat Northup helped me become consistent in my explanations, helped me aim the text at the audience I wished, and gave *many* other helpful comments. Leslie Gorsline gave many suggestions and in general has helped my writing style over the years. Finally, Diana Northup has given me much needed support over the trials of writing which I have endured. I extend my deepest appreciation to these and all of the other people who assisted me with this endeavor.

# CHAPTER 1

# Introduction

## 1.1  Theme

The purpose of this book is to teach UNIX tool building by taking the reader through all facets of the design and implementation of a large, complete program. This book shows the reader the step-by-step development of *watcher*, a complete UNIX tool whose function is detailed later. By demonstrating new concepts in the context of this large program, rather than introducing concepts via isolated examples, the reader should get a clearer grasp of how these concepts relate to one another. By using existing UNIX tools to develop *watcher*, the reader gains a better understanding of these tools, as well as the insight that this "modular" strategy reduces the amount of time spent coding and debugging. This approach not only results in new useful tools, it also reinforces the concepts involved in their construction.

## 1.2  Tools

Within this book, a *tool* is a program, subroutine, or shell script which solves a general but well-defined problem. A tool differs from an ordinary program, subroutine, or shell script in its generality. It can often be reused in other contexts with little or no modification.

Consider the following example: You need to watch several computers more or less simultaneously, with the goal of averting problems before they occur. One possible solution would be to connect one terminal to each computer and move between the terminals continually, watching each system. Obviously, this arrangement wastes both terminals and time. To save time you could automate the process by creating a list of areas to watch and having each machine send you the status of each item via electronic mail. This solution is better, since it requires only a terminal at which to read your mail. Unfortunately, you are still doing most of the work.

An even better solution would be to write a program which can take a list of commands to run, along with a definition of what is "normal" or "acceptable" output for these commands, and have the program notify you only when something is wrong or "abnormal." This program can be used not only to watch an operating system, but anything for which "normal" can be defined. This is an example of a tool.

As another example, suppose you have a large program split into many files of code and you need to know from how many places the subroutine **printargs** is called in this program. No tools exist on UNIX specifically designed for this purpose; however, the tool *egrep* searches files for a pattern. Another tool, *wc*, counts the lines, words, and characters in its input. These two tools can be combined to produce the desired information by using a powerful concept known as a *pipe*, where the output of one program serves as the input for another. A pipe is analogous to an assembly line, where the workers receive parts, perform their tasks with the parts, then send them down the line to the next worker. In the example about finding the number of times a subroutine is called, the following command line would produce the answer[1]:

```
egrep 'printargs(.*);' *.c | wc -l
```

With pipelines, there is little need for temporary files. On many operating systems, a command is run with the output going to a file. A second command is run with the file as its input. The pipeline is a much cleaner and more elegant solution to the problem.

Many tools are written under the assumption that they will be used as part of a pipeline. They read from the standard input, modify or use the data in some way, then write it to the standard output. For example, *troff* is good at formatting text, but the *troff* commands needed to produce a table are low-level and difficult to use. The tool *tbl*, on the other hand, recognizes certain constructions as tables and produces the *troff* code necessary to produce a table. It changes only the part of its input which pertains to tables, and the rest is passed through unchanged.[2]

1. Don't worry if this seems confusing—it will be covered in more detail in Chapter 8.
2. Programs which change part of their input and pass the rest unchanged are often known as filters.

Programs designed to use and be used in pipelines tend to be more general than those programs not designed with pipelines in mind; that is, they can solve a wider range of problems than ones which were not designed with pipelines in mind. For example, *egrep* can search for patterns in one or more files or in data which comes from the output of other programs. These other programs may be working with devices (such as *tar* or *cpio*) or simply files. All of this variety of input requires little special design effort; the program is designed to read data from standard input, no matter what is actually generating the data.

A tool does not need to be a program; a subroutine can also be a tool. As with a program, a subroutine written as a tool should solve a general problem. It can then be used in other parts of the program or even in other programs with little or no modification, saving both coding and debugging time.

When writing a subroutine to be a tool, it helps to keep the routine short, making it easy to understand the whole purpose of the routine and also easier to debug it. Understanding all of the pieces and how they interact is key to understanding how the whole functions; short routines greatly aid this process.

Shell scripts can also be tools. On UNIX, the standard shells are programmable; programs written in the shell's language are known as shell scripts. These scripts can be used to solve problems by using other programs or shell scripts. They need to meet the same criteria as programs to be considered tools.

## 1.3   Rationale for Using UNIX

In the strictest sense of the word, UNIX refers to the kernel—the central core of the operating system which controls the computer and divides the resources among the users. However, in most cases, when people refer to UNIX, they mean not only the kernel but also the tools usually provided with UNIX—tools such as *grep*, *awk*, and the C compiler. When "UNIX" is used in this book, this broader definition is intended.

UNIX makes writing programs easier by providing many tools which help in building new tools. Since it was written by programmers for programmers, it has one of the richest toolkits available. Here is a brief introduction to some of these tools, as well as other general terms used frequently in the UNIX environment. They will be covered in more detail later in the book.

awk   A programming language which helps with data manipulation by doing part of the work (such as breaking the input up into fields) and allowing the programmer to easily express transformations to the data. *awk* can also be useful for prototyping ideas quickly to test their feasibility before doing a full implementation in a compiled language. *awk* was named for its authors: Alfred Aho, Peter Weinberger, and Brian Kernighan.

lex   Assists in building lexical analyzers (scanners) by taking a description of how to break the input into logical units (known as tokens) and generating C code for a routine which reads the input and returns the tokens found. *lex*-generated scanners are usually easier to modify than those written by hand.

yacc   Takes up where *lex* leaves off; given a grammar describing a language it generates C code for a parser for that language. Parsers generally pose problems, but *yacc* makes them easy to write and modify.

make   Given a list of file dependencies, *make* rebuilds only the files which are out of date (such as object files depending on source files; if a source file is newer than its corresponding object file, *make* will recompile it). *make* saves programmer and CPU time.

shells   The "outer layer" of the operating system. The user interacts with the operating system through a shell; the shell reads input from the user and executes commands. On UNIX, several shells are available. In addition to handling the redirecting of I/O to files or down pipelines, a shell is often also a programming language in its own right.

mail   On UNIX, *mail* has several user interfaces available, and it can be used to communicate with people on the local machine, within a site, or across the world through a network.

USENET   A loose network of computer systems—most running UNIX—that exchange electronic news and mail. There are many discussion groups "on the net," and information on a multitude of technical and nontechnical topics can be found among them. The technical groups are good places to learn more about UNIX (or any other topic).

UNIX also provides support for the programmer from the operating system itself, via system calls and library functions. The system calls provide access to the raw power of the operating system; the library functions make some of this power available without burdening the programmer with too many details. The services provided by these system calls and library functions range from doing I/O to keeping track of and communicating with other processes in the system (or across a network).

With UNIX few decisions are already made for the programmer; almost anything can be changed (although it might take a little work). With this programmer's freedom of choice comes the programmer's responsibility to pass this flexibility on to the user. If the programmer makes decisions for the user, this has the effect of limiting the applications for which the program is useful; the resultant program might prove inadequate for applications unforeseen when the program was written. In this case, the program would have to be modified, or else a new program must be written to handle the new situation. The most useful tools are those which make the fewest *a priori* assumptions.

UNIX is available for more types of computers than any other operating system. It runs on everything from personal computers through the Cray supercomputers. Programs written for UNIX can usually be moved easily between machines made by different vendors.

There is much public-domain or inexpensive (often free) copyrighted software available for UNIX. This is due in part to UNIX's long history of use at universities where software is often given away after it is written. This software usually comes complete with source code, allowing the user to learn and make modifications (or fix bugs). This book follows the tradition by providing source which may be freely copied without royalties (see the copyright page for full information about the copyright on *watcher*).

## 1.4   Scope of the Book

Throughout this book it will be assumed that the reader is familiar enough with UNIX to know how to use one of the editors provided. Also necessary is at least an acquaintance with the C programming language and knowledge of how to use the C compiler provided with the system.

### 1.4.1   Background Information

On UNIX, there is the concept of standard I/O. When a shell starts any program, it has associated with it three I/O streams: input, output, and error. (These are commonly referred to as **stdin, stdout,** and **stderr,** pronounced "standard in," "standard out," and "standard error.") When a program reads without specifically referring to a file, it reads from the standard input. Similarly, when it writes without a reference to a specific file, it writes to the standard output. By default, all three streams are connected to the controlling terminal (the terminal which initiated the process). With the shell, the input or output may be redirected to or from files (via > or <) or through a pipeline. The standard error is normally still attached to the controlling terminal even if the standard output is redirected; this allows error messages to be seen immediately, instead of disappearing down a pipeline or into a file.

As mentioned earlier, the shells on UNIX are programmable. A program written in a shell is usually called a shell script. Writing shell scripts is covered in Chapter 9.

## 1.4.2 Additional Resources

Since no one book can cover everything, the reader is directed to several books which provide information complementing the information this book presents. In Section A.4 of Appendix A is a bibliography listing these and all other books referenced throughout this book.

- Marc Rochkind's *Advanced UNIX Programming* goes into detail about the system calls and the concepts needed to understand them and also gives several small examples of how to use them.
- *The UNIX Programming Environment* by Brian Kernighan and Rob Pike is a good (but somewhat dated) introduction to using many of the tools that UNIX has to offer. It stresses the use of tools to solve problems whenever possible.
- The classic book on programming in C is *The C Programming Language* by Brian Kernighan and Dennis Ritchie, the developers of the language. It is the best reference book available for the language. Recently, a new edition was released which describes the ANSI standard for the C language. From here on (and elsewhere in the UNIX community), this book will be referred to as K&R.
- For more information about writing tools, *Software Tools* or its close relative *Software Tools in Pascal*, both by Brian Kernighan and P. J. Plauger, are unmatched.

The reader might also find some of the software available from the Free Software Foundation useful. Dedicated to the philosophy that source code should be available to all, the Foundation's products all come with source code and may be obtained directly from the Foundation or from anyone who has a copy. The products available are well written. Support is minimal, but since the source is provided, problems can be tracked by investigating the source.

The software available includes (but is not limited to) a C compiler and debugger, a C++ compiler, a parser generator similar to *yacc* (*bison*) and the editor *emacs*. For more information, contact the Free Software Foundation at the following address.

> Free Software Foundation, Inc.
> 675 Massachusetts Avenue
> Cambridge, MA 02139
> (617) 876-3296.

## 1.5  Organization of the Book

This book covers all stages of program development: design, coding, debugging, documentation, and use.

Designing tools is covered in the second chapter, including an overview of the problem to be solved, the criteria which must be met in a solution, and the initial design of the system.

The next three chapters cover the tools used to implement the solution. These tools are lexical analyzers (including the use of *lex*), *yacc*, and *make*.

Chapter 6 goes into more detail about writing easy-to-maintain code and debugging hints. These hints include

- pretty-printing the control file [producing a nicely formatted (pretty) version of the control file] to verify that the lexical analyzer and parser are functioning correctly before continuing with the coding
- a verbose option which shows what is happening elsewhere as the rest of the program runs
- debuggers such as *dbx* which pinpoint where and why core dumps occur, watching the executing of the program, and being able to examine variables at any point in the execution
- the use of appropriately placed **printf** statements

Chapter 7 discusses methods of writing proper documentation.

Next, in Chapter 8, the use of the example program *watcher* is covered. This includes interactions with other tools and useful commands such as *awk*, *wc*, *sort*, and *ps*. Both Berkeley and System V versions of commands will be discussed where appropriate.[3]

Chapter 9 covers the writing of shell scripts, and Chapter 10 describes the use of *watcher*.

---

3. Hopefully, these version differences in UNIX will disappear soon.

Appendix A discusses sources of more information, including other books, how to use the UNIX manuals, learning by experimenting with small programs, and using USENET to obtain information.

After the main text, the complete source for the program developed (*watcher*) is provided in Appendix E. The paper presented at the summer 1987 Usenix conference describing *watcher* is given in Appendix D.

## 1.6   Portability Issues

UNIX and C are often hailed as a very portable combination. It is true that a C compiler exists for virtually every major computer available today. While UNIX is available for many machines, it comes in several versions. C compilers also differ in what extensions they offer and in how the "fine print" of the language is implemented. To help facilitate the process of moving programs between machines, the C language has been standardized by an ANSI committee. Additionally, work is being done by Unix International and the Open Software Foundation to create a UNIX standard.

Whether or not a program can be easily moved from one machine to another depends on the specific application. Routines such as device drivers tend to be hardware specific and hence will likely need modification in order for them to run on different computers. However, a general sort routine written in C could be moved between computers with no modifications, assuming it was well written.

The portability of programs also depends on the programmer. Many C compilers provided by vendors have extensions and library functions which are not universally available. The degree to which the programmer isolates the machine and system dependencies and adopts the tool approach is probably the most important factor in portability. If dependencies are not isolated, the whole program must be searched for machine- or system-dependent code when it becomes necessary to port the program to another machine. In addition to wasting time and energy, this greatly increases the likelihood that problems will be overlooked.

## 1.7   Conventions Used in This Book

To help make the topics under discussion clearer, several fonts will be used. Names of commands will be set in *italics*. Files and subroutine names will be in **boldface.** Examples that show what would be typed in at a terminal or in a file are in a monospaced font.

In the example programs, keywords will be **bold,** comments in *italics*, and the rest will be in the normal (roman) font.

Whenever an example is given, unless specifically noted, it should work on both Berkeley's version of UNIX and UNIX System V, with either *csh* or *sh*. The output may vary, as the commands and their output are not identical among the various versions of UNIX.

# CHAPTER 2

# Overview of the Problem and Its Solution

In solving any problem, the first step is to get an overview—to know what, specifically, the problem is. This chapter discusses the problem that led to the development of the program, *watcher* (the reasoning for this name will become apparent shortly), presented in this book as an example of UNIX tool building. Also covered is the background of the problem, criteria for a solution, and methods which were considered as solutions but later rejected. Finally, the overall design of *watcher* is presented, with a special note on designing debugging aids as part of the program.

## 2.1 Background of the Problem to Solve

At the University of New Mexico, the number of computers that the systems group maintained was growing while the number of staff was not. In order to have time to do tasks such as evaluating new hardware and software or developing new software, a person was selected on a rotating basis who would carry a beeper and solve any emergency problem that came up on the systems. This person, affectionately known as "DOC," had the support of the rest of the group, but was the primary contact for any problems.

The goal of this process was to catch problems before users noticed them. To help meet this goal, we identified the most commonly occurring problems:

- running low on or out of disk space
- users who started programs with infinite loops and then put them in the background since they were taking a while to execute

- daemon processes which died, multiplied, or started using lots of CPU time
- machines crashing
- computers having problems communicating on the campus-wide communications network

Shell scripts were written to run programs (such as *ps*) and the output was mailed to DOC. These shell scripts ran every six hours, producing a great deal of output which DOC had to sift through looking for problems. The problem with this approach was that most of the time things were normal; DOC spent a lot of time reading mail looking for problems when there were none.

A cycle built up; something new was found which might develop into a problem. The shell script would be modified to watch it. This produced more output so the script would be tailored to produce as little as possible while still watching for the problem. Then, yet another potential problem was identified.

UNIX comes with many powerful tools for program development, but none of these simply watch the system for signs of trouble. Programs like *ps* and *df* provide information regarding the current state of the machine, yet it still remained DOC's responsibility to interpret this information and assess the health of the system at any given time. The problem can be solved by providing the system with the capacity to determine its own state of health, advising DOC only when it notices a potential problem requiring intervention.

## 2.2  Criteria for a Solution

A program which would help DOC had to be flexible enough to watch anything that the current on-call person considered important. With the shell scripts, if a new problem was discovered, a new command would be added and then when the script ran, DOC would scan the additional output. Any new solution needed to be able to be changed quickly and easily.

Flexibility, while a necessary criterion, was not sufficient. In order to improve DOC's effectiveness, the program should run frequently, catching the problems early. Also, *watcher* should be as silent as possible, except when it detects a potential problem. Any advantage gained by using the program would be lost if *watcher* delivered verbose status reports. The reports needed to be exact and concise, leading DOC immediately to the problem.

Finally, the solution should be a tool. It should not be tied to system administration, but capable of watching anything for which "normal" or "abnormal" can be defined.

## 2.3 Potential Solutions

The first solution considered was redesigning the shell scripts currently in use. After all, they were working; the only problem was the amount of output. With tools available such as *awk* (for a description of *awk*, see Section 8.6), the output of *df* (the amount of free disk space) could be monitored by the following pipeline:

```
df -i | tail +2 | awk '$5 >= 90 || $8 >= 50'
```

which would print out only those lines of *df -i* which indicated disk partitions more than 90% full or whose total inodes used were greater than 50%. The *tail +2* removes the header from the *df* output. Figure 2.1 shows the output of *df -i* on a Berkeley UNIX system. The result of the pipeline is shown in Figure 2.2. This solution did succeed at reducing the output from *df*.

A problem with this solution was that DOC would not notice a change between two DOC reports of a filesystem which was filling up rapidly but was not at 90% of capacity. It is also questionable whether DOC would remember the previous values.

Additionally, a different *awk* script was necessary for each program. Watching some things, such as the daemons, and seeing if their CPU time had changed by a significant amount since the last run,

| Filesystem | kbytes | used | avail | capacity | iused | ifree | %iused | Mounted on |
|---|---|---|---|---|---|---|---|---|
| /dev/hp0a | 7415 | 6033 | 640 | 90% | 567 | 1289 | 31% | / |
| /dev/hp2h | 140488 | 99007 | 27432 | 78% | 11196 | 27716 | 29% | /usr |
| /dev/hp0d | 7419 | 2673 | 4004 | 40% | 365 | 1491 | 20% | /usr/spool |
| /dev/hp0h | 140488 | 70916 | 55523 | 56% | 8478 | 30434 | 22% | /u4 |
| /dev/hp0e | 148143 | 114926 | 18402 | 86% | 14906 | 26054 | 36% | /u1 |
| /dev/hp0f | 52431 | 39825 | 7362 | 84% | 11359 | 5025 | 69% | /usr/man |
| /dev/hp1d | 7419 | 145 | 6532 | 2% | 15 | 1841 | 1% | /tmp |
| /dev/hp1h | 140488 | 87220 | 39219 | 69% | 9132 | 29780 | 23% | /u3 |
| /dev/hp1e | 148143 | 58942 | 74386 | 44% | 8423 | 32537 | 21% | /usr/src |
| /dev/hp1f | 52431 | 42813 | 4374 | 91% | 5591 | 10793 | 34% | /develop |
| /dev/hp2a | 7415 | 9 | 6664 | 0% | 4 | 1852 | 0% | /apswap |
| /dev/hp2d | 7419 | 4010 | 2667 | 60% | 230 | 1626 | 12% | /usr/spool/mail |
| /dev/hp2e | 148143 | 88078 | 45250 | 66% | 8209 | 32751 | 20% | /u5 |
| /dev/hp2f | 52431 | 25566 | 21621 | 54% | 4602 | 11782 | 28% | /u2 |

**Figure 2.1**  Output of *df -i* on a Berkeley UNIX system.

| /dev/hp0a | 7415 | 6033 | 640 | 90% | 567 | 1289 | 31% | / |
| /dev/hp0f | 52431 | 39825 | 7362 | 84% | 11359 | 5025 | 69% | /usr/man |
| /dev/hp1f | 52431 | 42814 | 4373 | 91% | 5591 | 10793 | 34% | /develop |

**Figure 2.2**  Output of df -i | tail +2 | awk '$5 >= 90 || $8 >= 50' when the output of *df -i* is as in Figure 2.1.

would be difficult. A program to generate these *awk* scripts could be written, but this would represent a complex solution for a simple problem.

## 2.4  The Solution

The best way to solve this problem is to look at what DOC actually does when he or she scans the output of the shell scripts. How exactly does DOC spot the potential problems present in the DOC report?

The output which DOC is watching is the output of pipelines such as *df, ps -ax | sort* (or on System V, *ps -e | sort*), and *ruptime*. Determining if a problem existed was a matter of scanning this output, and deciding if

- a number has exceeded a maximum or minimum value
- a number has changed too much from the previous run, assuming that the previous run was remembered
- a string value is not an acceptable value (for example, a machine was "down")

Basically, DOC knows what values are "normal" and takes action whenever these values are not normal.

Getting a program to do the scanning of the output is more difficult than might appear at first glance, due to inconsistencies in the location of pertinent information between runs of these commands. For example, the process occupying the fifth line of *ps -ax* might appear the next time on the eighth line; similarly, *uptime* does not consistently put germane information in the same place on the line for each invocation (it depends on how long the machine has been up).

What is consistent among the output of programs is that the pertinent information appears in either

- the same columns
- the same fields, where a field is a group of characters separated by white space, counted from the left
- the same fields counted from the right

*watcher* needed to be able to parse the output of programs in all of these ways (note that parsing the output of these programs is still easy compared to parsing the control language).

For specifying what is normal, the following definitions are used:

- a string value was in a list of acceptable values
- a numeric value was within an acceptable range
- a numeric value did not change by too large a percentage between runs
- a numeric value did not change by too much

Rather than have *watcher* execute with arguments telling it what to expect as input, it uses a file from which it reads (a control file). This file contains information on which pipelines to run, how to parse their output, and what is normal. A control file was chosen over command line arguments since more information is needed than conveniently fits on a command line.

The problem of reading the control language lends itself well to the use of a parser. *watcher* needs to be able to tell the infinite number of legal control files from the infinite number of illegal ones. The language is complex enough that the parsing could be difficult.

The control language is similar to a programming language (although a limited one), and the program *watcher* acts as an interpreter for that language. However, the results of running *watcher* depend not only on the "program" but on the state of the system when it is run.

In coming up with the syntax for the control language, clarity and ease of parsing were priorities. A language is easy to parse if it can be easily broken into tokens without having to look ahead into the input, and if the structure of the language can be described by a grammar that *yacc* can use.

First, we have to be able to specify a pipeline to execute. To make it easy to find the end of the pipeline (a pipeline may span more than one line and include most any character) parentheses ( ( and ) ) surround it. For example:

```
(df -i | tail +2)
```

After specifying the pipeline, we need to know how to parse the output. As mentioned previously, this takes two forms: column and field. The difference between the two must be easy to determine. Fortunately it is not difficult, since to specify something which has a start and an end column, we need two numbers, while to specify in which field an important piece of information occurs we need but one.

Therefore we can specify output between specific columns by a range such as 5−7, and a field by a single number such as 4.

Knowing where to find the important pieces of output is not sufficient. Somehow it is necessary to connect portions of the output with the specifications of what is normal. The easiest way to relate the parsing with the description is to label each item with a character string. At this point, an entry which tells *watcher* that the first field in the output of *df -i | tail +2* is the filesystem would look like:

```
(df -i | tail +2)
1 filesystem
```

It is also necessary to know what kind of data to expect in these fields or columns. A similar idea already exists on UNIX elsewhere: **printf,** the standard I/O library function from C. The specifications for printing data exceed what we will need. For consistency with what people who program in C are used to using, we can use %d to represent integers, %f to represent floating point numbers, and %s to represent strings.

Not used in **printf** is %k. Since we will need to be able to key on a certain part of a line for comparisons in the next run, this will be how we specify these keys. When *watcher* runs, it matches results from the previous run (if there was one) to the current run by looking for lines with identical keys.

To put everything together which has been discussed so far, we could have an entry in the control file to look at the output of *ps,* watching for processes which have used more than some number of CPU minutes. Output from a *ps -ax* command on a Berkeley UNIX system is presented in Figure 2.3. An entry in the control file as designed so far would look like (the control file is for a Berkeley-style *ps,* but the idea is similar for System V):

```
(ps -ax)
1-6 pid%k 20-22 minutes%d
```

which says that the process id (labeled pid) is found in the first through sixth columns of the output. The minutes of CPU time are in the 20th through 22nd columns of the output. Presumably this will be referenced in the section describing what is "normal."

Similarly, to give an example of field parsing, suppose we were watching disk usage. Output of the *df -i* command is presented in Figure 2.1. To watch both the free disk space (to make sure that it does

| PID | TT | STAT | TIME | COMMAND |
|---|---|---|---|---|
| 0 | ? | D | 0:26 | swapper |
| 1 | ? | S | 8:10 | init |
| 2 | ? | D | 0:13 | pagedaemon |
| 63 | ? | S | 11:56 | /etc/syslogd |
| 70 | ? | S | 82:44 | /etc/routed |
| 74 | ? | S | 16:39 | /etc/named /etc/named.boot |
| 79 | ? | I | 44:49 | /usr/lib/sendmail -bd -q15m |
| 87 | ? | S | 0:34 | /usr/lib/mand |
| 145 | ? | S | 24:41 | /etc/update |
| 148 | ? | I | 7:52 | /etc/cron |
| 156 | ? | S | 80:46 | /etc/rwhod |
| 160 | ? | S | 2:48 | /etc/inetd |
| 165 | ? | I | 0:35 | /usr/lib/lpd |
| 188 | ? | IW | 0:00 | - std.9600 ttyS3 (getty) |
| 1591 | co | I | 0:03 | -csh (csh) |
| 1622 | co | I | 0:01 | oper |
| 2095 | ? | I | 0:00 | - std.9600 ttyS8 (getty) |
| 5586 | ? | I | 0:00 | - std.9600 ttyS5 (getty) |
| 5808 | ? | I | 0:00 | d1200 ttyd2 (getty) |
| 5822 | ? | I | 0:00 | - std.9600 ttyT4 (getty) |
| 29864 | Se | Z | 0:00 | \<defunct\> |
| 5338 | d0 | I | 0:08 | -lsh (lsh) |
| 5778 | d0 | S | 0:08 | vi diff.out |
| 5857 | d0 | S | 0:00 | sh -c ps -ax |
| 5858 | d0 | R | 0:00 | ps -ax |
| 23235 | d0 | T | 0:20 | rn |
| 5021 | d1 | S | 0:04 | -csh (csh) |
| 5859 | d1 | S | 0:00 | mail cscbrkac@charon |
| 3679 | p0 | I | 0:08 | telnetd |
| 3680 | p0 | I | 0:02 | -csh (csh) |
| 4922 | p0 | I | 0:00 | /usr/local/bin/oper |
| 5777 | S4 | I | 0:01 | -csh (csh) |
| 5800 | S4 | S | 0:02 | rn |

**Figure 2.3**  Output of ps –ax on a Berkeley 4.3BSD system. (The output has been edited to allow it to fit on one page.)

not go above 90%), and the inodes[1] used (to make sure not more than 60% are used), we would need the following control file fragment[2]:

```
(df -i | tail +2)
1 filesystem%k 5 spaceused%d 8 inodesused%d
```

1. Inodes are file headers. They are discussed in detail in Maurice Bach's *The Design of the UNIX Operating System*, Prentice-Hall, 1986.
2. This example is assuming Berkeley-style *df* output. On System V, the idea is similar, but the output format and command line argument are different.

To make it easy to tell the end of the output format and the beginning of the change format, we need to choose a character which will separate the two sections. A logical choice is a colon (:).

Now that we can specify the pipeline and how to parse the output, we will need to specify what is "normal." Here is a syntax for each of the ways of specifying what is "normal" listed above:

- to verify that a string value is in a list of acceptable values:

  name "string1", "string2"

- to tell if a numeric value is within an acceptable range:

  name lower upper

  where lower and upper are numbers
- to specify a normal percentage change:

  name value%

  where value is the maximum percentage change considered "normal"
- to specify absolute changes:

  name value

  where value is the largest absolute change allowed with the definition of "normal"
- to specify that no change is allowed:

  name.

To make the parsing of the individual entries in the change format easier, we shall use a separator between the individual items. The semicolon (;) has traditionally been used as a separator in programming languages, and it will work well here.

Finally, to tell we have reached the end of an entry, we will end it with a period (.).

Every language should support comments. Following a convention which exists in many programs on UNIX, a pound sign (#) begins a comment and a newline ends it.

To sum up, Figure 2.4 has entries to watch disk space and processes. The first entry watches the output of the *ps* program, reporting any processes which have used more than 10 minutes of CPU time. The second entry checks the disks, looking for rapid changes in a filesystem or one which is close to full.

```
# CPU time should not be above ten minutes (we have
# a machine running student programs).
(ps -ax)
1-6 pid%k 20-22 minutes%d:
        minutes 0 10.


# disks should be less than 90% full and have less than
# 60% of the inodes used. Also, any change of more than
# 15% should be noted.
(df -i pipe tail +2)
1 filesystem%k 5 pctused%d 8 pct_inodesused%d 3 blocksused%d:
        pctused 0 89;
        blocksused 15%;
        pct_inodesused 0 59.
```

**Figure 2.4**   Sample control file for *watcher*.

The generation of the parser for this language is covered in Chapters 3 and 4.

## 2.5  **Coding of** *watcher*

In *watcher*, most of the subroutines are one page long or less, and each subroutine has one well-defined task. Longer subroutines tend to do too much, making bugs more likely. It is easier to test a subroutine designed to do only one thing and do it well than it is to test a subroutine which tries to do many things.

While subroutine calls incur overhead, in general, the programmer time saved by using them is greater than the CPU time spent executing them. In cases where optimization of the CPU time is more important, a C compiler which can handle inline subroutines[3] should be used; Part II of Jon Bentley's *Programming Pearls*[4] or all of his *Writing Efficient Programs*[5] should be consulted.

*watcher*'s parser is produced by *yacc*. Without *yacc*, parsers are difficult to write and even harder to maintain or expand. Section 4.1 gives an example of how easy it is to enhance parsers written with *yacc*. Besides *watcher*, an example which expands dates in the form *month/day/year* (i.e., 8/5/89) to *month day, year* (i.e., August 5, 1989) is given in Section 4.6. This program could be modified easily to

3. *gcc* from the Free Software Foundation can do this.
4. Addison-Wesley, 1986.
5. Prentice-Hall, 1982.

change any date it saw into the long format. Or, the idea of parsing dates could be used to write a program which takes the times of day that people are unable to get together for a meeting and produce a list of the times which everyone can make. With *yacc*, a program such as this can read any date format and does not need to be long or complex.

The data structure which *watcher's* parser builds is complex. It contains three levels of nested structures, some of which are connected in linked lists. Each of these levels corresponds to a subroutine, so the subroutine receives a part of the structure, deals with its level, and relies on lower level subroutines for dealing with lower levels of the structure. This one-to-one correspondence maintains a sane approach to dealing with this complexity. The structure itself is discussed in more detail in Section 6.2.

C programming style has some idiosyncrasies which do not occur in other programming languages. For example, it is a common practice to make an assignment of a value from a function in an **if** statement, using the value later on if there was no error returned. Many functions return a code indicating success or failure while modifying one or more of their arguments (functions with side effects). This style runs against what has been taught in other programming languages, but it is the way C programs are written, and it can produce clean code.

In programs written by the author, each subroutine is in its own file. This creates lots of files but reduces the compile time when only one subroutine has been changed, and it makes finding the routines easy.[6] *make* takes care of knowing which files need to be recompiled (*make* is discussed in detail in Chapter 5).

## 2.6 Debugging

A program such as *watcher* should be written in stages, and each stage should be tested thoroughly before proceeding to the next. With this method of development, bugs are most likely to exist in the new code and not in the already-debugged code.

---

6. A file of "tags" that tells in which file and at what line routines are defined can be created, and both *vi* and *emacs* can use this information to find routines quickly also. See the manual page ctags(1), i.e., the manual page for ctags found in Section 1 of the *UNIX Programmer's Manual.*

Any large program contains bugs (as do many small ones); most of the time spent programming is actually spent debugging. This debugging time can be reduced if thought is given to debugging when the program is designed—that is, designing debugging aids as part of the program.

The first stage for *watcher* is to get the parser for the language functioning, in order to build data structures encoding the information contained in the control file in a format that the rest of the program can use. A debugging aid that helps here is to have the program produce a clean, pretty version of the control file. If we can pretty-print the control file (which should be parsable!), then it is likely that the parser is building the data structures correctly. Since there is no telling when the ability to verify the parser will cease to be useful, it was left in *watcher* as an option.

As work proceeds on *watcher,* we will be working on the part which reads and parses the output of the pipelines. For assistance in debugging this section, we will add a verbose option which will have *watcher* print what it read from the pipeline and how it was broken into interesting parts. This debugging aid will be useful after *watcher* is written in order to see differences between what was expected in the output of the pipelines *watcher* runs and what is actually read from them.

Additional debugging hints are scattered throughout the book, close to relevant topics.

## 2.7  Portability Issues

*watcher* uses *yacc* to generate the parser for the control file, which limits the compilation of *watcher* to those machines which have *yacc*. While this may seem a small limitation since almost all UNIX systems have *yacc*, very few other systems have it.[7]

There are differences between System V Release X and Berkeley 4.X systems. Two which affect *watcher* are the maximum lengths of file names, and the names of some of the library functions. File name lengths are kept unique below the System V limit of 14 characters.[8]

---

7. The bison parser generator, available from the Free Software Foundation, is a *yacc*-compatible parser which can also run on VMS.
8. This restriction will be removed with System V Release 4.0.

The C preprocessor construction "#ifdef SYSV" is used to select the appropriate names for the library functions (such as *index* versus *strchr*).

*watcher* does not use any system calls directly, so incompatibilities between various dialects of UNIX here do not cause problems.

## 2.8 Summary

The goal of *watcher* was to reduce the amount of time necessary to watch a system for possible problems. By defining what is "normal," the user of *watcher* can keep tabs on anything that can be done with a pipeline.

A program should be written in stages, debugging each stage before moving on to the next. In *watcher*, the first stage was getting the parser functioning, followed by the portion which checked output for being within the limits specified in the control file.

*watcher* makes use of small subroutines, each of which has a single task and is in a separate file. This practice saves the programmer time when used in conjunction with *make*.

Finally, *watcher* has been run on both Berkeley UNIX and UNIX System V, so it is an example of a portable program.

# CHAPTER 3

# Lexical Analysis

## 3.1 Background

Figure 2.4 was a short example of a file which could be used to control what *watcher* does (a control file). The first task in writing *watcher* is to read this file and make some sense out of it (parsing). The first step in parsing is lexical analysis, the subject of this chapter.

The contents of this control file are similar to a program written in an interpreted programming language, which is then run by the interpreter. In the case of *watcher*, the language is not as powerful as a programming language; it only controls what the program *watcher* does.

Reading a control file can be much more difficult than may appear at first. We have this file full of data which is structured in some way. Somehow, we have to take this data and turn it into something that the program can use. The first step is to break the file into pieces, each of which is a logical unit (known as a token). In a programming language, these units are items such as keywords, integers, floating point numbers, and operators. In *watcher*'s case, they are items like pipelines, strings, or punctuation. This is lexical analysis, the subject of the present chapter. These tokens must then be assembled into something which makes sense to the program. This is parsing, which is the subject of Chapter 4.

Lexical analysis and parsing can be compared with an automobile factory. In one end come raw materials which are combined to make various subassemblies such as fenders, engines, and seats. This is the job of a lexical analyzer. The parser is like the rest of the assembly line, taking these units and putting them together to form the final product.

Lexical analysis is often a relatively simple task. All that is needed from a lexical analyzer is the ability to recognize simple structures (the tokens) in the input. UNIX provides a tool, *lex*, which assists in the process of writing the lexical analyzers (sometimes also known as scanners). However, since the task is simple (as in the case of *watcher*), a lexical analyzer can often be written without *lex*. This chapter will first discuss scanners which do not use *lex*, then it will cover *lex* and how to use it. Lexical analyzers which use *lex* are slightly easier to maintain or change, and the more you know about lexical analyzers, the easier it is to use *lex*. Covering both methods will allow you to compare and contrast the two methods of generating lexical analyzers and choose the most appropriate method for your problem.

Besides the *watcher* lexical analyzer, other examples using *lex* will be given.

## 3.2 *watcher*'s Lexical Analysis Needs

The *watcher* control language has fairly simple lexical analysis needs (compared to a programming language). Tokens for *watcher* consist of the following characters:

; " : % - . , { }

(the braces will be explained later in Section 4.1), but also include items such as identifiers (or strings) and pipelines. Tokens sometimes are more than just a simple logical unit. While a PIPELINE is a token, it also has a value—the string containing the pipeline to execute. Everything in the *watcher* control file is either a simple token from the list of characters above, a string, a pipeline, or a number (either floating point or integer).

The ease of writing a lexical analyzer depends on the language being parsed. Some languages need to look ahead into the input to determine what kind of token has been found. The *watcher* control language requires no lookahead for lexical analysis; upon seeing a character one can determine what kind of token it is (or is part of). If lookahead is needed, *lex* makes the job easier. *lex* is covered in Section 3.4.

## 3.3 The Non-*lex* Lexical Analyzer for *watcher*

The lexical analyzer written for *watcher* (Figure 3.1, **yylex.c**) is very straightforward. The routines it calls appear in Appendix E where the entire source for *watcher* is presented alphabetically by file type then by file name.

```
/* Cyylex.c
yylex for watcher: this is a simple routine looking for numbers,
special characters and strings. The special chars are stored in
'words' and represent tokens by themselves. In y.tab.h are the
values to return for the various tokens which are not listed in
'words'.

Kenneth Ingham

Copyright (C) 1987 The University of New Mexico
*/

#include "defs.h"
#include "y.tab.h"

char words[] = "\".,*|;:%@$-{}";

yylex()
{
        int c, i;
        static char str[MAX_STR];
        int real;

        while (isspace(c = getchar()))
                ;

        if (c == EOF)
                return EOF;

        if (c == '(') { /* aha, pipeline */
                c - getchar();
                for (i=0; c != EOF && c != ')'; i++) {
                        str[i] = c;
                        c = getchar();
                }
                str[i] = '\0';
                if (c == EOF) {
                        fprintf(stderr, "Missing ')' to end pipeline.\n");
                        return EOF;
                }
                yylval.str = strsave(str);
                return PIPELINE;
        }

        if (c == '#') { /* comment to end of line */
                while (c != '\n' && c != EOF)
                        c = getchar();
                if (c == EOF)
                        return EOF;
                return yylex();
        }

        if (index(words, c) != 0)
                return c;
```

**Figure 3.1** Lexical analyzer for *watcher*. (*Figure continues.*)

```
if (c == '+' pipepipe c == '-' pipepipe isdigit(c)) { /* a number */

        real = False
        i = 0;
        str(i++) = c;

    do {
        str(i++) = getchar( );
        if (str[i-1] == '.')
            real = True;
    } while (isdigit(str[i-1]) pipepipe str[i-1] == '.');
    (void) ungetchar(str[i-1]);
    str[i-1] = '\0';
    if (real) {
        yylval.real = (float) atof(str);
        return FLOAT;
    }
    else {
        yylval.integer = atoi(str);
        return INTEGER;
    }
}

if (c == '\'') { /* literal string */
    c = getchar( );
    for (i=0; c != EOF && c != '\'; i++) {
        str[i] = c;
        c = getchar( );
    }
    str[i] = '\0';
    yylval.str = strsave(str);
    return STRING;
}

/* nothing else matched. Must be plain string (whitespace sep) */

for (i=1, str[0]=c; c != EOF && !isspace(c) && !index(words,c); i++) {

    c = getchar( );
    str[i] = c;
}
(void) ungetchar(c);
str[i-1] = '\0';
                    yyval.str = strsave(str);
                    return STRING;
            }
```

**Figure 3.1** (Continued)

Whitespace (tabs, spaces, and newlines) is not significant in the control language, so it may be used to make the file more readable. Therefore, we skip over any whitespace which comes before a token. **isspace** is a macro contained in the include file **ctype.h** which returns nonzero (true) if its argument is whitespace. It is documented in section three of the *UNIX Programmer's Manual* under **ctype** (from here on, this will be abbreviated by **ctype(3)**).

Note that no matter what character is seen, as the lexical analyzer looks for the end of the token it also checks for end-of-file. The necessity of always checking for possible errors cannot be stressed enough. Even "impossible" errors should be checked; the "impossible" does happen.

**yylex** handles comments in an interesting way. Since the next line may start with a # and therefore also be a comment, the code necessary to watch for this could get quite messy. A much easier and cleaner method is to call a routine which already knows how to deal with a comment—**yylex.** This is an example of an important concept in both lexical analysis and parsing—recursion. If the next line is not a comment, then the token returned by the recursively called **yylex** will be returned by the original invocation. Otherwise we continue recursively, ignoring the comment and looking for the next token. When the last of the recursively called **yylex**s returns, the recursion "unwinds," and the token found is passed to the calling instance of **yylex,** which in turn passes it on to its caller and on up the line.

Recursion is a useful and powerful concept. In many cases, a problem can be reduced to a simpler version. This reduction continues until a simplest case is found, known as a base case. A common example of this is the factorial function, $f(n)$. This function is the product of all of the integers from 1 to $n$. An iterative solution in C is in Figure 3.2. A recursive solution is in Figure 3.3. Note how the problem is reduced to the base case (when $n == 1$), and a method for making the problem smaller is given in the second **return** statement.

```
factorial(n)
int n;
{
        int f, i;

        f = 1;
        for (i=2; i<=n; i++)
            f = f * i;
        return f;
}
```

**Figure 3.2**   Iterative factorial function.

```
factorial(n)
int n;
{
        if (n == 1)
              return 1;
        else
              return n * factorial(n-1);
}
```

**Figure 3.3**  Recursive factorial function.

This is a characteristic of recursion. Recursion will be used for more complex tasks in Chapter 4 which covers parsing.

With any recursive call (or any loop, for that matter), we need to be sure of the termination conditions. In **yylex,** the recursion will end as soon as the end of file or a token is seen. Unless a file of infinite length consisting of nothing but comments is seen (an unlikely occurrence), the recursion will terminate and unwind. Some overhead is incurred by the recursion. In any normal control file this is minimal since comments are broken up by tokens.

## **3.4**  *lex*

*lex* is a tool provided with most UNIX systems and it makes writing lexical analyzers easier. The input for *lex* is a collection of regular expressions along with fragments of code, which are executed when input matching the regular expression is found. *watcher* uses a *lex*-generated lexical analyzer most of the time (the other scanner is kept only for testing and teaching).

### 3.4.1  Regular Expressions

*lex* is one of many programs which use regular expressions (others include many of the editors such as *ed, ex, sed,* and *vi* in which regular expressions are used in the substitutions and searching and the pattern searching program *egrep* which searches for lines which match the given regular expression). The syntax for the regular expressions is similar for all of the UNIX programs, but the specific *lex* syntax will be discussed here.

Regular expressions allow one pattern to match many strings. Because of this, in an editor, fewer changes may need to be specified; the regular expression can consolidate them into one. In a pattern searching program, one pattern can match all of the strings of interest. In some cases, all strings of interest may not be known; all that is known is that they have a certain structure. Regular expressions can then be used to find all of the strings of interest.

A regular expression consists of a collection of characters which may match many different strings. The simplest regular expression is a single character (with a few "special" exceptions discussed below). It matches only itself. For example, the regular expression

y

matches only the character y.

More complex regular expressions are built by concatenating several smaller regular expressions. In a simple example, the regular expression

abc123

matches only the string abc123 anywhere in the input stream.

Regular expressions have several characters which modify an expression or match more than one character. The first and most important to remember is the backslash (\). It removes the special meaning of any character following it. To match a backslash, the following regular expression could be used:

\\

In *lex* only, quotation marks (") may also surround regular expressions—all characters within the quotation marks are without special meaning.

A caret or circumflex (∧) placed at the beginning of an expression forces the match to be at the beginning of a line. For example,

∧abc123

matches abc123 only if it is at the beginning of a line.

Similarly, a dollar sign ($) matches the end of a line, so

abc123$

will match abc123 only if it is at the end of a line.

Therefore, to match a line consisting of only the string abc123, the following expression could be used:

∧abc123$

A dot ( . ) matches any single character. Continuing with the example we have been using, the regular expression

ab.123

matches the strings abc123, abz123, ab9123, ab!123 *ad infinitum.* It does not match strings such as abcd123.

A class of characters may be defined by enclosing them in brackets ( [ and ] ).

[zyxa]bc123

matches only the following strings: zbc123, ybc123, xbc123, and abc123. Within the brackets, most of the characters lose their special meaning; the only ones which remain special are discussed next.

Rather than specifying every character, if the range of characters is consecutive in the character set used by the computer (in most cases, this is ASCII, in which the character ranges a through z, A through Z, and 0 through 9 are consecutive), the sequence may be specified by the starting and ending characters with a dash (-) between them. For example, a regular expression matching any single digit is

[0-9]

If a class of characters includes the dash (such as in negative numbers), it must be the first or last character. For example,

[-+0-9]

would match all of the digits and the two signs.[1]

A caret (∧) at the beginning of a class complements the characters listed. So

[∧a-zA-Z]

matches any character which is *not* an upper or lower case letter.

Finally, in character classes, a backslash ( \ ) can be used to remove the special meaning of any character.

---

1. This example was taken from the paper *Lex—A Lexical Analyzer Generator* by M. E. Lesk and E. Schmidt. A copy of this paper is provided along with the documentation for most UNIX systems.

The star or asterisk (*) matches zero or more occurrences of the previous regular expression. Therefore

a*bc123

matches bc123, abc123, aabc123, and aaaaaaaabc123, among many.

Similar to a star is the plus sign (+) which matches one or more occurrences of the prior regular expression. The expression

a+bc123

matches abc123 and aabc123, but does not match bc123.

If an arbitrary number of occurrences of a prior regular expression like the star and plus sign is too general, a certain number of repetitions may be specified:

w3,5

matches only www, wwww, and wwwww (this only works with *lex*).

Regular expressions may be grouped using parentheses ( ( and ) ). The expression

(abc123)+

matches one or more occurrences of the string abc123.

To match one of several expressions, the vertical bar ( | ) is used to separate the expressions. So

abc|123

would match the strings abc or 123. If this expression were part of a larger expression, the parentheses would be needed for grouping:

(abc|123)xyz

matches either abcxyz or 123xyz.

An expression may have an optional part which is indicated by a following question mark ?. For example,

abc(123)?def

matches abcdef and abc123def. Note the use of parentheses for grouping.

To tie all of this together, here is a more complex regular expression:

```
^re+(re)*gular ((e|z)xpression)? \$[0-9]
```

This expression matches many strings. Among them are

```
regular expression $0
rerereregular $7
rererererererereregular zxpression $3
```

A string which is not matched is `regular ezxpression $5`.
   Table 3.1 has a summary of all regular expressions.

## 3.5   *lex* **Input Files**

A *lex* input file has three sections. These are declarations, rules, and subroutines sections, separated by lines consisting of only %%. Hence an input file looks like:

```
declarations
%%
rules
%%
subroutines
```

The declarations and subroutines sections are optional. A minimal *lex* input file would look like:

```
%%
rules
```

where the rules are pairs of regular expressions and code to execute when the regular expression is matched in the input. The rules will be discussed in detail in Section 3.5.2.

### 3.5.1   The Declarations Section

The declarations section is used to set up the environment for the lexical analysis. One example is to define a name for a pattern to make the rules easier to write. In the declarations section, lines of the form

*name translation*

**Table 3.1**
Summary of Regular Expressions

| Character or example | Matches |
| --- | --- |
| *Any nonspecial* | Itself |
| y | y |
| \ | Removes special meaning of next char |
| \* | * |
| "*chars*" | *chars* |
| "*" | * |
| ∧ | Beginning of line |
| ∧abc123 | abc123 at beginning of line |
| $ | End of line |
| abc123$ | abc123 at end of line |
| . | Any single character |
| ab.123 | abc123, abz123, ab9123, and more |
| [*chars*] | Any of the *chars* listed |
| [zxa]bc123 | zbc123, xbc123, and abc123 |
| [*char1*-*char2*] | Any character between *char1* and *char2* |
| [0-9] | 0, 1, 2, 3, 4, 5, 6, 7, 8, and 9 |
| [∧*chars*] | Any of *chars* not listed |
| [∧a-zA-Z] | Any nonletter |
| * | Zero or more of prior expression |
| a*bc123 | bc123, aabc123, aaaabc123, and more |
| + | One or more of prior expression |
| a+bc123 | abc123, aaaabc123, and more |
| exprnum1, num2 | num1 through num2 occurrences of *expr* |
| w3,5 | www, wwww, and wwwww |
| (*expr*) | expr |
| (abc)+ | abc, abcabc, abcabcabc, and more |
| *expr1*|*expr2* | *expr1* or *expr2* |
| abc|123 | abc or 123 |
| *expr*? | *expr* or nothing |
| abc(123)? | abc or abc123 |

First case listed is general and then an example is given.

```
%{
/* sample lex declaration section */

#include "y.tab.h"

extern int fubar;
%}

digit [0-9]
letter [a-zA-Z]
```

**Figure 3.4**  Sample declarations section for a *lex* input file.

associate *name* (any string of characters with the first character in the first column) with *translation* (a regular expression).[2] For example, the following definition:

```
digit [0-9]
```

associates with the name `digit` with an expression matching any digit. This definition may be used in a later regular expression (including one in the definitions section) by referencing the name in braces ({ and }). For example:

```
[-+]?{digit}+.{digits}*
```

will match any decimal number, assuming numbers less than one and greater than negative one have a leading zero and that a decimal point is always written.

The declarations section can also include lines containing only %{ and %}, which delimit text to be copied into the *lex*-generated program and to be external to the function **yylex.** Examples of things which can go between these lines are C preprocessor directives (such as #define) and external variable declarations.

A sample declarations section is in Figure 3.4.

2. A bug exists in some versions of *lex* which prevents ∧ and $ from working in an alias like this. A construction like

```
comment      ∧#.*$
%%
{comment}    { eatcomment(); }
```

will fail, but

```
comment      #.*
%%
∧{comment}$  { eat comment(); }
```

will work. Thanks to Stephen Friedl for pointing this out to me.

### 3.5.2 The Rules Section

The rules section consists of lines of the form:

*expression code*

where *expression* is a regular expression as described in Section 3.4.1 and *code* is a program fragment to be executed when the expression is matched. When **yylex** is being used with **yyparse** (the parser generated by *yacc*), these program fragments often consist of a simple **return** statement, returning the appropriate token. Refer to Section 4.4 for more information about the combined use of *lex* and *yacc*.

The action may also need to know what string matched the pattern (e.g., for saving the string to be used in some other part of the program). This string is stored in the array **yytext**. A *lex* pattern and action which uses this could be

```
[a-zA-Z][a-zA-Z0-9]*    { strcpy(id_name, yytext);
                           return IDENTIFIER; /* an integer */
                         }
```

which recognizes an identifier, saves the string in the variable **id_name,** and then returns the token IDENTIFIER so that the parser knows what type of token was seen.

*Ambiguities*

If the input string can be matched by more than one pattern, the longest match is chosen. For example, with the rules

```
abc[a-z]* { code1 }
abcd      { code2 }
```

the input string abcdefg will match the first pattern and *code1* would be executed, even though part of abcdefg would also match the second pattern. If two rules both match the longest pattern, then the rule appearing first is used.

This action by *lex* can cause problems for the unwary programmer who uses constructions such as .*. For example,[3] to match a string within ticks ('), one might be tempted to use the pattern

```
'.*'
```

---

3. This example is based on one in *Lex—A Lexical Analyzer Generator*, by M. E. Lesk and E. Schmidt.

However, this would not always match the desired way. With

```
the subroutine 'fubar' is a palindrome
```

as input, the expression '.*' would have the desired effect of matching 'fubar'. However, with the input string

```
the routines 'fubar' and 'foo' were written to be ...
```

the expression '.*' would match the string <u>'fubar' and 'foo'</u> since it is the longest. A regular expression which would have the desired effect is

```
'[^']*'
```

which works by matching everything except a tick (') which appears between ticks.

*Input Which Matches No Pattern*

In *lex*, if input is seen which matches no pattern, it is copied to the standard output. If this could be a problem, a "catch-all" pattern should be included to pick up anything not matched by the other rules. A pattern with a null action [nothing except a semicolon (;)] causes that pattern to be ignored; an example of this is

```
[ \t\n]+            ; /* white space - ignored */
```

which causes whitespace (spaces, tabs, and newlines) to be ignored.
   The echoing of characters which are not matched by any expression makes debugging easier—any character which appears unexpectedly is one which was not properly taken care of.
   This echoing of unmatched characters can also be useful when *lex* is not used with *yacc*, but is used by itself as a program to transform data in some way. In these programs, the actions may be more complex. For example, a *lex* program to expand tabs into spaces (**extabs.l**) is shown in Figure 3.5. *extabs* reads from the standard input, expands the tabs into spaces, and then writes the result to the standard output.[4] Specifically, any character which is not a tab or a newline is simply sent to the standard output (via the **ECHO** command which is supplied by *lex*). If a tab is found, it is expanded to the next tab stop

---

4. Programs such as *extabs* which pass their input through to their output making some changes along the way are often called filters.

```
%{
/*
extabs: a lex program to expand tabs.

Assume tabs are every 8 columns.
*/

#include <stdio.h>

int column = 0;
%}

%%
\t { do {
                putchar(' ');
                column++;
                } while ((chars % 8) != 0);
        }
[^\n\t] { column++; ECHO; }
\n { column = 0; putchar('\n'); }
```

**Figure 3.5**   *lex* program which expands tabs into spaces.

(which is assumed to be every eight characters). Finally, the last line of the example matches the newline and resets the character counter so we know how many characters are on the line for expanding.

### 3.5.3   Using *lex*

**extabs.l** would be compiled by the following sequence of commands:

```
lex extabs.l
cc -o extabs lex.yy.c -ll
```

*lex* produces a file with C subroutine in it (plus anything you put in the programs section) named **lex.yy.c.** This file must then be compiled with the C compiler. The –11 on the *cc* command line loads in the *lex* library, simply a **main** which calls **yylex** and a version of **yywrap** which tells *lex* what to do when it finds end-of-file.

### 3.5.4   *lex* and I/O

When **yylex** gets an end-of-file indication, it will call the function **yywrap.** If **yywrap** returns 0, more input is assumed to be available and **yylex** continues reading. If it returns 1, **yylex** wraps up and returns 0 as the token (which happens to be an endmarker for *yacc*).

   The *lex*-generated scanner reads from the standard input unless the special routine **input** is redeclared. **input** is a macro, so it may be redefined in the declarations section. Another alternative is to reopen the file pointer **stdin,** a good use for the routine **yywrap.** For example, Figure 3.6 has an updated version of *extabs* which reads from files or the standard input. If it is reading from files and finds end-of-file, it opens the next file provided and continues expanding tabs in it.

### 3.5.5   The Subroutines Section

Everything following the %% which separates the rules from the subroutines is copied into the output program. Subroutines called by **yylex** may be placed here (like in Figure 3.6). This section is optional. If it is not included, the %% may be left out also (which is the case in Figure 3.5).

## 3.6   Using *lex* **with** *yacc*

When *yacc* calls **yylex,** it expects **yylex** to return an integer representing the token seen. The patterns in *lex* match tokens for the parser, and the normal action is to return the proper token, possibly saving the value for use by the parser. A simple example would be

```
,         return ',';
[0-9]+    return INTEGER;
```

In the first case, the token returned is the integer value of a comma ( , ), in the computer's character set. In the second, INTEGER is a constant which was defined via a **#define** (more about this later when *yacc* is covered).

For a more complex example, in a lexical analyzer looking for integers the following line may be used:

```
[0-9]+              { push(atoi(yytest)); return INT; }
```

which takes the string matched by the pattern (which is stored in the array **yytext**), pushes it onto a stack, then returns the token identified (in this case, an INT).

However, a better way exists. In Chapter 4, *yacc* pseudo-variables will be introduced. The lexical analyzer can return values for these pseudo-variables also by placing the value in the variable **yylval.** In the same vein as above,

```
[0-9]+              { yylval = atoi(yytext); return INT; }
```

```
%{
/*
extabs: program which expands tabs. Can handle command line args
telling which files to work with.

Assume tabs are every 8 columns.
*/

#include <stdio.h>

int column = 0;
char **av;
int ac, arg;
%}

%%
\t { do { putchar(' '); column++; }
            while ((column % 8) != 0); }
[^\n\t] { column++; ECHO; }
\n { column = 0; putchar ('\n'); }

%%

main(argc, argv)
char *argv[];
int argc;
{
        if (argc > 1) {
                if (freopen(argv[1], "r", stdin) == NULL) {
                        perror(argv[1]);
                        exit(1);
                }
        }
        av = argv; ac = argc; arg = 2;

        (void) yylex();
}

yywrap()
{
        if (arg < ac) {
                if (freopen(av[arg], "r", stdin) == NULL) {
                        perror(av[arg]);
                        exit(1);
                }
                arg++;
                return 0;
        }
        return 1;
}
```

**Figure 3.6** Updated version of *extabs* which can read from files supplied.

will return the value of the token as well as what type of token it is. **yylval** is defined in the file **y.tab.h** and is by default an integer. Changing its type is discussed in Section 4.4.

## 3.7 The *lex* **Input File for** *watcher*

The input to *lex* for a lexical analyzer for *watcher* is in Appendix E; its filename is **control.l**. It is short since the lexical analyzer for *watcher* is simple.

The first patterns in the lexical analyzer for *watcher* are the one-character tokens which can be quickly identified. Two entries watch for numbers and two watch for strings of various types. Note that looking for a string in ticks ( ' ) is similar to looking for a pipeline; in both cases, the regular expression will match only up to the first terminating character seen [either a tick ( ' ) or a right parenthesis ( ) )].

The lexical analyzer counts the newlines it sees so that a line number can be provided when error messages are generated, making the determination of errors easier when the parser produces error messages.

Note that *watcher* has two lexical analyzers supplied in Appendix E—one for use with *lex* (**control.l**) and one without *lex* (**Cyylex.c**). *watcher* runs the same way with either one. Both are supplied to provide a contrast between *lex*-generated scanners and those written by hand. To switch from the *lex* version to the one written in C, the file **Cyylex.c** would have to be copied to **yylex.c** and the **Makefile** modified so that it does not try to use the *lex* version.

## 3.8 Summary

At this point we have two ways of breaking the control file into tokens. Without using *lex*, a C program identifies the tokens. *lex* offers the benefit of an easily modified scanner. Regular expressions define the tokens, and code fragments tell *lex* what to do once they have been recognized.

*watcher* now has the ability to read control files and break them up into tokens. To make sense of the tokens, we need a parser, the subject of the next chapter.

# CHAPTER 4

# Parsing the Control File

## 4.1  Background

At this point, we have a lexical analyzer returning tokens representing the logical units of the input file (such as the control file for *watcher*). The next step is to make sense of these tokens. This is the job for the parser.

A parser has two purposes. First, it checks the syntax of the input language. If the input is not syntactically correct (i.e., the tokens cannot be put together to make a structure, as in the C expression a+++++++b), it is difficult, if not impossible, to determine what the user meant.[1]

The second and more important role for the parser is to identify the structure represented by the input. It is then up to the rest of the program to make some sense out of this structure. In most cases (as with *watcher*), the parser builds a data structure which represents the input, and the program uses this information to determine what to do.

Parsers written without the assistance of a compiler-compiler or parser-generator are often large and hard to modify. With most UNIX systems the tool *yacc* (*Yet Another Compiler Compiler*) is provided, which makes writing parsers easier than writing them from scratch. *yacc* allows you to concentrate on the structure of the language being parsed, while it does the grunge work of identifying the structure. As an added benefit, parsers written with *yacc* are easy to modify.

Parsers are useful whenever the input which will be read is structured and can be described by a grammar (a formal way of specifying the structure of the input). They are not limited to programming lan-

---

1. Even when the input is syntactically correct, it is often not what the user meant.

guages—examples of programs which use parsers include

1. **calendar utilities** for parsing dates and/or actions.
2. *make* for reading its control file describing how to build programs and files (see Chapter 5 for more information on *make*).
3. *eqn* (a program which formats equations for use with *troff* or *nroff*) for recognizing the *eqn* constructions for building the equations.
4. *watcher* for its control language.

Here is an example of how easy it is to modify parsers written with *yacc:* When *watcher* was first written, in any report of something which was not normal the entire pipeline was used in the report of the problem. Some of these pipelines were a bit long and cluttered the output (some examples are in Chapter 10). The solution was to create an "alias" to be used instead of the pipeline when reporting a problem. The following syntax was chosen: After the pipeline a string can be placed in braces ({ and }) which will be used in the report of any problems. Use of an alias is optional, and if it is not supplied, the pipeline itself will be used in the reports.

To make the change to *watcher* to allow aliases was simple. An entry for the alias was added to the command structure, and in the *yacc* grammar file, 14 lines were added and one was modified. Finally, the section which produces the reports was modified to use the alias if supplied.

*yacc*'s input is a file with a grammar in it. A grammar is a set of rules describing the structure of the input. For example, the grammar for a natural language such as English is a set of rules describing the structure of the phrases, clauses, and sentences in the language. A grammar can also describe the expressions, control flow, and routines for a programming language (like C).

*yacc* produces a file, **y.tab.c,** containing a parser (**yyparse**) which then must be compiled with the C compiler.[2] In the case of *watcher,* this parser also builds the data structure used by the rest of the program to do the job of watching. In other cases, such as the date-expander presented in Section 4.6, the parser acts immediately.

*yacc* produces parsers for LARL(1) grammars. For an in-depth description of this and other grammars along with much more detail about parsing in general, good references include *Principles of Compiler Design* by Alfred V. Aho and Jeffrey D. Ullman,[3] and *The Theory*

2. *yacc* can produce parsers for other languages, but they are beyond the scope of this book.
3. Addison-Wesley, 1977.

*of Parsing, Translation, and Compiling, Volume I: Parsing,* also by Aho and Ullman.[4] The original reference for *yacc* is *Yacc: Yet Another Compiler Compiler* by Stephen C. Johnson; this paper should be included in the documentation available for your system. This paper contains additional information about advanced *yacc* concepts which will not be covered here.

## 4.2   The *yacc* **Grammar File**

As in *lex*, a *yacc* grammar file contains three sections:

```
declarations
%%
rules
%%
subroutines
```

The declarations are similar in concept to the *lex* declarations but are specific to *yacc*. They will be covered in the next section. The rules are the *yacc* grammar rules, and the subroutines section is copied to the output in the same way as it the subroutines section of a *lex* input file.

## 4.3   *yacc* **Rules**

A *yacc* grammar rule has the form

*rule* : *body* ;

The rule is the name for the structure described in the body. For example,[5] the rule

```
date : month day ',' year ;
```

says that a date is composed of a month, a day, the character ' , ' and a year. Note that what comprises a month has not been specified; it could be an integer between 1 and 12 or it could be a string such as Jan or January. More on this in a moment.

---

4. Prentice-Hall, 1972.
5. This example is based on one in *Yacc: Yet Another Compiler Compiler.*

This rule can recognize

January 1, 1970

as a date, assuming that month is either a token returned by the lexical analyzer or the name of a rule which recognizes month names.

The dividing line between the lexical analyzer and the parser (which is first mentioned in Section 3.5.2) is not well defined. In the above example, month could be a token (returned by the lexical analyzer), or it could be the name of a *yacc* rule, as in:

```
month : 'J' 'a' 'n' 'u' 'a' 'r' 'y' ;
month : 'F' 'e' 'b' 'r' 'u' 'a' 'r' 'y' ;
                .
                .
                .
```

which would result in a very simple lexical analyzer (which does nothing but return letters and punctuation as tokens). It is best, however, to let the lexical analyzer do as much of the recognizing as possible, since using the parser wastes time and space and also may make the grammar too complex for *yacc* to handle.

The names of tokens and rules may be as long as necessary and are composed of letters (upper and lower case letters are distinct), dots ( . ), underscores ( _ ), and digits (digits may not start a name, however). Tokens may also be literals—characters enclosed in ticks ( ' )—such as the ' , ' in the rule describing date above. A literal may also be one of the C character escapes such as ' \n ' for a newline or ' \xxx ' where xxx is the octal value for a character in the machine's character set. This form is useful when nonprinting characters, such as tabs, are an integral part of the syntax; they can be specified in a way that allows easy identification. Additionally, transfer between machines is easier since all of the characters in the grammar file are normal, printing characters.

Tokens are integers, and the parser needs to know their values, hence they must be declared (in the declarations section). The easiest way to declare tokens is

```
%token name1 name2 name3 . . .
```

In this case, *yacc* will generate unique token numbers for all of the tokens. If *yacc* is run with the –d flag, it will write these token numbers as **#define**s to the file **y.tab.h** which can be included in other C

source files. In particular, if this file is included in the lexical analyzer, when the lexical analyzer discovers a token, it returns the name
of the token (which was defined in the include file). It is unnecessary
to know the actual values of the tokens. All of the examples in this
book, along with *watcher*, use this method of token number generation.

The token numbers may be declared by the user, in which case the
numbers follow the names on the %token line(s). For example,

```
%token identifier 34 month 25 target 235
```

says that when the lexical analyzer returns a 34, the token is identifier, a 25 is month, and a 235 is a target. The ability to define your
own token numbers can be useful when they are constrained by some
other portion of your program. A better solution, however, is to use
the variable **yylval** (discussed in Section 3.5.2 and Section 4.4) for
passing semantic information from the lexical analyzer to the parser;
its use may result in a cleaner parser.

Several grammar rules may have the same name (as the month example above shows); a shorthand for this notation is

```
name :  body1
     |  body2
     ;
```

where a vertical bar (|) separates the various bodies from each other.

The parser tries to find a structure which represents the first rule
(the start rule). If you wish to use a rule other than the first, it must be
specified in the declarations section by a line like:

```
%start name
```

where *name* is the name of the rule to where parsing should start.

Parsing stops when **yyparse** receives the endmarker from the lexical analyzer. If all of the tokens up to the endmarker form a structure
which matches the start symbol (i.e., in a parser recognizing dates, a
date), the parser is said to accept the input and **yyparse** returns 0.
Otherwise it rejects the input and **yyparse** returns 1.

The endmarker is a token whose value is less than or equal to zero.
Remember this if you define your own token number—do not define
one to have a value <= 0. Doing so will cause the parser to act oddly[6]
and it is a difficult error to discover.

---

6. IBM refers to this behavior as "unpredictable results."

With each grammar rule, you can have an action to be performed when the rule is recognized. These actions may be any C code and can accomplish useful tasks such as building structures. In *watcher*, the actions build the structure representing the control file. In other parsers, the actions may do something immediately. For example, a schedule-checking program that reads days and times to find out when people are busy may have actions which mark as busy the days/times parsed.

Actions are specified by one or more C statements enclosed in braces ({ and }). For example:

```
date : month day ',' year
      {$$ = date ($1, $2, $4) ; }
    ;
```

(The odd variables which begin with dollar signs ($) are discussed in the next section.)

## 4.4 Pseudo-variables

The dollar signs in the above example show another feature of *yacc*. With each rule, a value is associated. The value that a rule returns can be set by setting the pseudo-variable $$ to some value in the action (such as the value returned by the function **date** in the above example). Values returned by rules are available by using the pseudo-variables $1, $2, etc. Still using the same example, the value returned by the rule month is associated with $1, day with $2, and year with $4. If a rule does not explicitly return a value, the value of the first element is returned (equivalent to an action of { $$ = $1 }).

These values may also be returned by the lexical analyzer, associating a semantic value with the token. The lexical analyzer can assign a value to the external variable **yylval;** this value is then available in the parser as a pseudo-variable. For example, suppose in our lexical analyzer we have the following fragment:

```
            .
            .
            .
"January"   {yylval = 0; return MONTH; }
"February"  {yylval = 1; return MONTH; }
```

```
"March"         {yylval = 2; return MONTH; }
"April"         {yylval = 3; return MONTH; }

                .
                .
                .
```

Then in the parser we could know what month was seen and use it as the index for an array:

```
                .
                .
                .

date:           MONTH DAY ', ' YEAR
                {
                        months [$1] [$2] = OK;
                        printf ("year: %d\n", $4) ;
                }
                .
                .
                .
```

Using pseudo-variables can eliminate the need for most other methods of transferring information between the lexical analyzer and the parser as well as between rules in the parser.

By default, the values of the pseudo-variables are integers, however *yacc* has support for arbitrary types. The stack on which the parser stores the values of the pseudo-variables can be a union of all of the types which may be encountered (i.e., strings for identifiers, the value of integers and floating point numbers, etc.). In this case, *yacc* will insert the appropriate union member names whenever the pseudo-variables are used; programs such as *lint* will not produce any messages about mismatched types. A union is declared by placing the following in the declarations section of the *yacc* grammar file:

%union { *body of union* }

Once the union has been declared, member names need to be associated with the rules. The keyword %type is placed in the declarations section:

%type ⟨*union-entry*⟩ *name1 name2* . . .

where *name1, name2,* . . . are names of tokens or rules.

```
%union {
        char string[15];
        int integer;
        float real;
}

%type ⟨integer⟩ month day year
%type ⟨real⟩    change maximum
%type ⟨string⟩  month_name
```

**Figure 4.1**  Simple example of %union and %type with *yacc*.

```
%{
#include ⟨stdio.h⟩

#define TRUE  1
#define FALSE 0

int debug = TRUE;
long start, end;
%}
```

**Figure 4.2**  Example using %{ and %} in a *yacc* grammar file.

In a simple example (Figure 4.1), the union contains either a **float** or an **int.** The tokens or rules[7] month, day, and year are all integers, while change and maximum are both floating point numbers. When month, day, and year are used in the rules, the pseudo-variables associated with them will use the union element integer. Similarly, the element real will be used for the pseudo-variables associated with a change or a maximum.

If *yacc* is run with the –d flag, the **typedef** for the union and a declaration for the variable **yylval** are placed in the file **y.tab.h.** Other variables can have the same type as the union by declaring them to be of type **YYSTYPE.**

Global variables can be declared, files **#include**d, and constants **#define**d (in the declarations section) by enclosing the declarations in %{ and %}. An example is in Figure 4.2.

Global variables should not begin with **yy** in order to avoid possible clashes with those used by the parser or lexical analyzer.

---

7. The example does not provide enough information to determine whether month, day, and year are tokens or rules.

## 4.5 Support Routines for *yacc*

The parser generated, **yyparse,** needs additional support to make a complete program. First, it needs a **main** to call it. Next, **yyparse** calls **yylex** to get tokens. If an error (most often a syntax error) is detected, the parser will call the routine **yyerror** with the text of the error message (a null-terminated string) as the argument. The simplest **yyerror** is one of the form

```
yyerror(s)
char *s;
{
        printf("%s\n", s);
}
```

which simply prints the error message on the standard output. A more complex version is demonstrated in Section 4.7 when error handling is discussed. Simple versions of **main** and **yyerror** are available in a library on most systems; to use them, add a -ly to the C compiler command line (an example of this is found in the next section.)

## 4.6 A Small *yacc* Example

Consider the *yacc* grammar (Figure 4.3) for *conv*, a program which recognizes dates of the form *month/day/year* and prints them in an expanded format. For example, 3/13/89 would be printed as March 13, 1989. The lexical analyzer uses *lex* and is presented in Figure 4.4. To turn these files into a program that will run, the following sequence of commands could be used:

```
yacc -d conv.y
cc -c y.tab.c
lex conv1.l
cc -c lex.yy.c
cc -o conv y.tab.o lex.yy.o -ly
```

The -ly on the last line loads in a main program which simply calls **yyparse** and then exits (it also has a version of **yyerror** but the one supplied in **conv.y** will be used instead). When executed, the result will be an executable file named **conv,** which reads from the standard

```
%token INT
%{
char *monthname[] = { "January", "February", "March", "April",
        "May", "June", "July", "August", "September", "October",
        "November", "December" };
%{
%%
dates: nothing          /* line 1 */
    | date              /* line 2 */
    | dates date        /* line 3 */
;

date: INT '/' INT '/' INT
        { expand($1, $3, $5); }
    ;

nothing: ;
%%
yyerror(s)
char *s;
{ printf("%s\n", s); }

expand(month, day, year)
int month, day, year;
{
        if (month < 1 || month > 12) badnum ("month", month);
        if (day < 1 || day > 31) badnum ("day", day);
        if (year < 1 || year > 99) badnum ("year", year);

        printf("%s %d, 19%02d", monthname[month-1], day, year);
}

badnum(what, value)
char *what;
int value;
{
        printf("Invalid %s: %d\n", what, value);
        exit(1);
}
```

**Figure 4.3**  **conv.y:** the *yacc* grammar for the date converter.

input until end-of-file. Any date of the form *month/day/year* is expanded. No other text matches the patterns, so it is echoed to the standard output by the lexical analyzer without being changed. An error message is produced if anything other than a date is provided which has slashes (/) or digits.

```
%{
extern int yylval;
#include "y.tab.h"
%}

%%
[0-9]+ { yylval = atoi(yytext); return INT; }
"/" return '/';

%%
yywrap()
{ return 1; }
```

**Figure 4.4**  conv.l: *lex* file for the date converter.

```
alias              : '{' STRING '}'
                   {
                           $$ = $2;
                   }
                   pipe empty
                           { $$ = NULL; }
                   ;
```

**Figure 4.5**  *yacc* rule from *watcher* which shows the use of the **empty** rule.

In the grammar file for *conv*, an interesting rule to note is the **nothing** rule, which states

```
nothing : ;
```

and matches an empty string. In *conv*, it allows a file with no dates to avoid a syntax error. In *watcher* a similar rule is used to allow an alias to be optional (Figure 4.5).

The **nothing** rule, however, introduces an ambiguity into the grammar. Remember, the parser is trying to find a structure which matches **dates.** When the first **INT** is returned by the lexical analyzer, either line 2 (the relevant lines are numbered in Figure 4.3) or line 3 could apply. In the case of line 3, the **dates** which was seen previously was a **nothing.** *yacc* will produce a parser which applies line 2.

When *yacc* processes the file **conv.y,** it will warn you of this ambiguity with the following message:

```
conflicts: 1 shift/reduce
```

If *yacc* is run with the −v flag it will produce a file, **y.output,** which shows which rule is ambiguous. In the case of **conv.y,** this ambiguity is harmless; the parser works correctly no matter which interpretation is taken. In other cases, the ambiguity may not be as benign. Ambiguities should be checked to ensure that the parser will function as expected. Further treatment of ambiguities is beyond the scope of this book; for more information about what is going on inside the parser and how it deals with ambiguities, see Johnson's paper on *yacc* and/or one of the books on parsing by Aho and Ullman.

A sample run of *conv* is in Figure 4.6.

Note that **dates** is defined as **nothing,** a **date,** or **dates** followed by a **date.** This declaration allows the parser to recognize zero or more dates. Without **dates,** the parser would give the error message "syntax error" if anything other than exactly one date was seen (since zero, two, or more dates would not match a single **date**).

This basic structure for defining something as one or more elements of a list will be seen frequently. The list is defined via left recursion, when the recursive call appears first or on the left, that is, in a construction of the form:

```
foo: foo more_stuff
```

Use of left recursion is encouraged since the parser *yacc* builds is smaller, and more importantly, the internal stack used by *yacc* could potentially overflow with a long list if right recursion was used.

The **main** for *conv* could also have repeatedly called **yyparse** to expand the dates. However, several potential problems are inherent

```
% cat conv.in
On 1/1/70, time began for UNIX and the clock has
been counting the seconds ever since. Ken Thompson and
Dennis Ritchie presented a paper on UNIX on 10/17/73.
% yacc -d conv.y
% cc -c y.tab.c
% lex conv.l
% cc -c lex.yy.c
% cc -o conv y.tab.o lex.yy.o -ly
% conv < conv.in
On January 1, 1970, time began for UNIX and the clock has
been counting the seconds ever since. Ken Thompson and
Dennis Ritchie presented a paper on UNIX on October 17, 1973.
%
```

**Figure 4.6**  Sample run of the date conversion program.

with this approach. First, the lexical analyzer does not know when it has seen the end of a date (after all, that is the job of the parser) so it does not send an endmarker. Second, **main** doesn't know when the end of the input has been seen. It is therefore much easier to use recursion in *yacc* parsers.

## 4.7 The *yacc* Grammar for *watcher*

The *yacc* file for *watcher* is large and illustrates many of the capabilities of *yacc*. It is presented in Appendix E (the name of the file is **control.y**). The overall goal of this parser is to take the control file and build a structure to be used by the rest of the program. This structure is declared in **defs.h;** the parser allocates space for the items in the structure (many items are arbitrary-length lists) and fills in the appropriate values.

The grammar was built in a top-down manner. First, the overall structure was defined (the command structure). Then the pieces which make up this structure are defined, followed by the parts of these pieces, etc. Building in this manner tends to generate well-formed, logical grammars.

The *yacc* file starts out by declaring all of the tokens. Following these definitions are external variable declarations for variables such as the pointer to the head of the linked list of commands and declarations for the subroutines which the parser uses. This section ends with the %union and %type lines described in Section 4.4.

The actions associated with each rule build and initialize the appropriate part of the structure. In some cases, these actions are complex or repeated and are handled by subroutines, making a cleaner grammar file.

Error handling in parsers is traditionally a difficult subject. Unfortunately, it is not much better with *yacc*. Error handling is covered in detail in Johnson's paper on *yacc;* only part of it will be covered here. *yacc* has a special token, **error,** which is placed in the grammar rules at points where errors can be dealt with. If it is followed by another token, when an error is detected, everything up to this token is ignored in an attempt to get back on-track and to provide any additional error messages. To make this a bit more concrete, consider an example from the *watcher* control file (Figure 4.7). In this example, if an error is detected, all input is ignored up to and including the next period (.) (the end of the structure for this pipeline). The parser continues,

54 / 4. Parsing the Control File

```
command            : one_command
          {
                  if (clist == NULL)
                          clist = $1;
                  else
                          printf("Bad error in the parser. \n");
          }
       |command one_command
          {
                  struct cmd_st *p;

                  if (clist != NULL) {
                          for (p=clist; p->next!=NULL; p=p->next)
                                  ;
                          p->next = $2;
                  }
                  else
                          clist = $1;
          }
       |error '.'
          {
          fprintf(stderr, "Command error ");
          fprintf(stderr,"near line %d\n", control_line);
          parse_error = True;
          }
        ;
```

**Figure 4.7**  Example from the *watcher* grammar showing error handling.

```
/*
yyerror: print out the errors for the parser. To be helpful,
we print the line number in the control file where the
problem occurred.

Kenneth Ingham

Copyright (C) 1987 The University of New Mexico
*/

#include "defs.h"
yyerror(s)
char *s;
{
        extern int control_line;

        fprintf(stderr, "%s on or near line %d\n", s, control_line);
}
```

**Figure 4.8**  **yyerror** for *watcher.*

scanning for other errors; it will return 1, indicating that it did not accept the input. The main program will then note this and terminate.

One idea which makes errors easier to locate is to have the lexical analyzer keep track of the line number in the file being parsed in an external variable. When the parser needs to print an error message, this line number is used. For example, the **yyerror** which *watcher* uses is in Figure 4.8. Besides printing the error message supplied by *yacc*, the current line number in the file is also given as an aid to determining the cause of the error.

A distinctive style is used in the control file, following that recommended in Johnson's paper on *yacc:*

1. Use all capital letters for token names and all lower case for rule names. Doing so allows you to tell at a glance whether a name is a token or a rule and where to look to see how it is defined.
2. Put grammar rules and actions on separate lines in order to make changes easier.
3. Put all rules with the same name together; put the left-hand side in only once and let the rest of the rules for the same name be separated by vertical bars. Line up all of the vertical bars (tabs make this easy). This format makes it easy to find where a given rule is defined.
4. Put a semicolon only after the last rule for a given name and put it on a separate line. This makes it easy to add rules or actions.

As mentioned in Section 2.6, *watcher* was brought up by first verifying that the parser was functioning correctly. The verification was accomplished by building in an option to pretty-print the control file. The code which pretty-prints the structure built by the parser generated by the *yacc* grammar is discussed in Section 6.2.

## 4.8  Summary

Parsers are routines which identify the structure in the input, then may call upon the rest of the program to act upon this structure. They can be written easily with the aid of the tool *yacc. yacc* reads a file containing a grammar describing the structure of the input and produces C code for a parser which will recognize that structure. Parsers built with *yacc* are easy to write and modify.

Now, *watcher* has a structure, built by the parser, which represents the control file. By now, the source code is complex enough that when changes are made, the effect of the changes may not be easy to determine (a change to the grammar file may change the token numbers that *yacc* writes to **y.tab.h** and modify the behavior of the lexical analyzer). Maintaining a program is the topic of the next chapter.

# CHAPTER 5

# Compiling and Maintaining the Code

## 5.1  Introduction

As mentioned earlier in Section 2.5, the *watcher* source has only one routine per file. This method of storage makes finding routines easy,[1] but knowing what has been changed after debugging or enhancement may be difficult. This is where the UNIX utility *make* comes in handy (and illustrates one more tool which UNIX provides to make a productive programming environment). In general, when one is working on a project, the process is one of[2]

1. think
2. edit
3. make
4. test

To use *make* you specify which files "depend" on others. For example, if you compile **program.c** to get **program.o**, then **program.o** depends on **program.c.** A more complex example is a *yacc* parser and a *lex* lexical analyzer which includes the **.h** file created by *yacc* so the lexical analyzer knows what constants to return to the parser as it sees the tokens. Here we have **lex.yy.o** depending on **lex.yy.c** which depends on **scanner.l** and **y.tab.h** which depends on **grammar.y.** Figure 5.1 gives a graphical view of the relationship between these files.

1. There is also a method known as using a **tag** file. See the manual page for *ctags* in Section 1 of the *UNIX Programmer's Manual* for more information.
2. This process was first mentioned in the paper on *make: Make—A Program for Maintaining Computer Programs* by S. I. Feldman. This document should be provided with the documentation for your system.

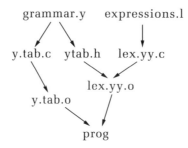

**Figure 5.1** Graphical view of the dependencies in a simple program using *lex* and *yacc*.

```
# prog depends on y.tab.o and lex.yy.o
#
# The line beginning with a tab tells how to build prog
# if either y.tab.o or lex.yy.o is newer than prog
prog: y.tab.o lex.yy.o
        cc -o prog y.tab.o lex.yy.o

# yylex.o depends on yylex.c and y.tab.h
lex.yy.o: lex.yy.c y.tab.h
        cc -c lex.yy.c

# In this rule, lex.yy.c is the target and it depends on
# expressions.l
lex.yy.c: expressions.l
        lex expressions.l

y.tab.o: y.tab.c
        cc -c y.tab.c

# note that there can be more than one target built by
# a rule
y.tab.h y.tab.c: grammar.y
        yacc -d grammar.y
```

**Figure 5.2**  Sample **makefile**.

It is in these complex relationships where *make* excels. To be able to keep the program up to date, no matter what has changed, and to only rebuild what is necessary, the **makefile** fragment in Figure 5.2 could be used (actually, most of what is in this **makefile** can be dealt with by *make*'s implicit rules, which will be covered in Section 5.2). The control file in which *make* looks for the dependency relationships is by default **makefile;** if it does not exist, *make* looks for **makefile.** If you do not wish to use either of these names, the control file

```
% make
yacc -d grammar.y
cc -c y.tab.c
lex expressions.l
cc -c lex.yy.c
cc -o prog y.tab.o lex.yy.o
%
```

**Figure 5.3**  Output when *make* is run with the **makefile** in Figure 5.2.

can be specified on the command line: `make -f makefile` where `makefile` is the name of the control file to use.

If *make* is executed with no target (the file to build) specified on the command line, it will make the first target found in the **makefile.** In Figure 5.2, the default target is `prog`. When *make* is run with this **makefile** in Figure 5.2, it produces the output which is in Figure 5.3.

When *make* runs, it checks the time when the target was last modified and when the files on which it depends were last modified. A target is considered up to date if

- all of the files on which the target depends are up to date
- the target is newer than the files it depends on

If a target is not up to date, the commands provided in the rule are executed, and no commands are provided, *make* implicit rules are used (implicit rules will be discussed in Section 5.2).

As illustrated in Figure 5.2, the *make* syntax is fairly straight-forward. A rule begins with a list of targets, a colon (`:`), and the files on which these targets depend. The lines following a rule which start with a tab instruct *make* how to build the target; as many lines as necessary can be used. The lines must begin with a tab. *make* uses the shell[3] to execute the commands provided.

## 5.2  Implicit Rules

*make* has a table of implicit rules which make writing **makefile**s easier. It knows about files listed in Table 5.1 (those that will be discussed in this book are `.c`, `.l`, `.o`, and `.y`). The implicit rules tell

---

3. Whether this is *csh*, *sh*, or some other shell depends on the version of *make* you are using and possibly which shell you have as a login shell.

**Table 5.1**
Suffixes for Files Which *make* Knows About

| Suffix | Type of file |
|--------|--------------|
| . c | C source files |
| . e | efl source files |
| . f | FORTRAN source files |
| . l | *lex* source files |
| . o | object files |
| . r | ratfor source files |
| . s | assembler source files |
| . ye | *yacc* efl-source files |
| . yr | *yacc* ratfor-source files |
| . y | *yacc* C-source files |

*make* how to convert any of the source files listed in Table 5.1 into an object file. If these are not sufficient for your task, you can add your own rules.

Rewriting the sample **makefile** in Figure 5.2 to make use of the implicit rules, we get the equivalent **makefile** fragment shown in Figure 5.4. When *make* is run with this **makefile,** it produces the output in Figure 5.5.

## 5.3   *make* **Macros**

### 5.3.1   User-Defined Macros

The YFLAGS = -d in Figure 5.4 illustrates another feature related to the implicit rules. When *yacc* is executed by *make*, it will pass the YFLAGS as arguments to *yacc* before the *yacc* source file on the command line. A similar macro exists for the C compiler (CFLAGS) and *lex* (LFLAGS). For example, if you want to include debugging information in with all C source files which are compiled, you could include the line

```
CFLAGS = -g
```

in the **makefile.** Another common use of the CFLAGS is to define constants with the -D option for the C compiler. For example, in the

```
YFLAGS = -d
prog: grammar.o expressions.o
        cc -o prog expressions.o grammar.o

# Note that the following lines all use make's implicit rules.
expressions.o: y.tab.h expressions.l

y.tab.h grammar.o: grammar.y
```

**Figure 5.4**   **makefile** using implicit rules.

```
% make
yacc -d grammar.y
/bin/cc -c y.tab.c
rm y.tab.c
mv y.tab.o grammar.o
lex expressions.l
/bin/cc -c lex.yy.c
rm lex.yy.c
mv lex.yy.o expressions.o
cc -o prog expressions.o grammar.o
%
```

**Figure 5.5**   Result of running *make* with the **makefile** in Figure 5.4.

*watcher* **makefile,** the operating system type (System V or Berkeley) is defined as a constant. The relevant fragment of the **makefile** is

```
SYSTEM = BSD
CFLAGS = -O -D$(SYSTEM)
```

Note that macros can be used in the definitions of other macros.

These xFLAGS are but a simple example of *make* macros. Macros can stand for items in the list of targets in the list of dependencies or be used in the commands to rebuild the target. Macros are defined by the following syntax:

*macro name = macro value*

A macro is referred to by $ followed by the macro name, or if the macro name is more than one character, by $ followed by the name in parentheses ( ( and ) ) or in braces ({ and }). An example which expands upon the **makefile** fragment we have been referring to is in Figure 5.6. Note the use of CFLAGS in the command to build prog, which guarantees any compilation flags are also used in the linking.

```
# flags to be used with the default rules
YFLAGS = -d
CFLAGS = -g
# object files needed to link into the program
OBJECTS = grammar.o expressions.o plain.o simple.o

# Note the use of the macro OBJECTS as the list
# of what prog depends on and in the list of
# commands needed to build prog.
prog: $(OBJECTS)
        cc $(CFLAGS) -o prog $(OBJECTS)

expressions.o: expressions.l y.tab.h

y.tab.h grammar.o: grammar.y
```

**Figure 5.6**   Sample **makefile** showing more macros.

Macros for *make* may also be specified on the command line. For example, make "CFLAGS = -O -DUNM" would override any definition of CFLAGS in the **makefile** and instead use -O -DUNM as the value for CFLAGS.

## 5.3.2   Predefined Macros

*make* has several "special" macros:

- $@ is the name of the target
- $? is the string of names which are younger than the target
- $* is the prefix shared by the current and the dependent file names
- $< is the name of the file which caused an implicit rule to be used

These macros allow one rule to describe how to build several files which share a common building method. Suppose a source control system such as *RCS* or *SCCS* is used to store and maintain versions of the source for a large project. To make the program, the source has to be obtained from the control system. With *RCS*, the following **makefile** fragment could be used:

```
SOURCE = foo.c fubar.c foobar.c

$(SOURCE):
        co $@
```

where *co* is the *RCS* command used to get a file from the revision control system. In *SCCS*, the **makefile** fragment would be

```
SOURCE = foo.c fubar.c foobar.c

$(SOURCE):
        sccs get $@
```

If the implicit rules are not sufficient to tell *make* how to build one type of file from another, you can provide this information. Lines of the form

```
.p.o:
        $(PASCAL) $(PFLAGS) -c $<
```

tell *make* how to convert .p files (presumably Pascal files) into object files (.o files). If you have a file whose suffix is not known by *make* (the list is in Table 5.1), the suffix can be added to *make*'s list by listing it as a dependency for the special target ".SUFFIXES." For example, if you had a C++ compiler which expected filenames to end in .C, a useful **makefile** fragment would be

```
.SUFFIXES: .C
C++ = g++

.C.o:
        $(C++) -c $(C++FLAGS) $<
```

which would inform *make* that .C was an interesting suffix and how to turn source files into object files.

As an example of when the special macro $? would be useful, consider the following **makefile** fragment from the *watcher* **makefile:**

```
print:: $(C_SRCS) $(H_SRCS) $(L_SRCS)
        $(PPRINT) -1C $?

print:: $(Y_SRCS)
        $(PPRINT) -lyacc $?

print::
        touch print
```

This fragment maintains an empty file called **print.** Every time the *make print* command is issued, it prints the files which are younger than the file **print** and then updates the date on **print** by *touch*ing it. The double colons separating the target from the files upon which it depends tell *make* that if the target is out of date with respect to any of the files listed, the commands provided are executed. Any target/ dependency list with a double colon may have commands associated with it. Only one target/dependency list can have commands in the single colon case.

When creating the examples for this book, the code was run through a pretty-printer. *make* ensured that the examples always matched the code. A **makefile** fragment which did this was the implicit rule:

```
.c.tex .l.tex .h.tex: ; $(LGRIND) -f $< > $*.tex
.y.tex: ; $(LGRIND) -lyacc -f $< > $*.tex
```

This example also shows one other feature of **makefiles**— instead of being on a separate line, the command(s) may be placed on the same line if a semicolon ( ; ) separates the dependency list from the command(s).

## **5.4**  *make* **"Tricks"**

### 5.4.1   Files Which Are Touched but Do Not Change

At certain times, a file may be regenerated but the contents may not have changed. An example of this is the file y.tab.h; every time *yacc* is run, a new version is created if the –d flag is given. If it has not changed, there is no need to recompile the files which depend on it. *make* does not have a built-in facility to deal with this problem, but an easy solution exists. Assuming *make* will use *sh* to execute the commands, the **makefile** fragment which deals with this problem is presented in Figure 5.7. (The **if** statement syntax will be discussed in detail in Section 9.5.1.) The idea here is to move the file to another

```
y.tab.h y.tab.c.c: control.y
        mv y.tab.h y.tab.h.old
        yacc -d control.y
        -if cmp -s y.tab.h y.tab.h.old: \
            then rm y.tab.h.old; \
            else mv y.tab.h.old y.tab.h; \
    fi
```

**Figure 5.7**   **makefile** fragment which does not touch **y.tab.h** unless it really changes, even if **control.y** changes.

name and then compare the new and old version, using the new version only if it is different. The *mv* command preserves the last modified time; a file which is only *mv*ed will be considered by *make* not to have changed.

### 5.4.2 Changing Directories

When *make* executes commands, a separate shell is used for each line. In most cases, no problem occurs with this method. However, it means that a *cd* command will have no effect on the following command. The easiest way around this limitation is to place the *cd* command on the same line as the command(s) which are to be executed in the other directory. For example:

```
library: lib/libfoo.a
        cd lib ; make libfoo.a
```

### 5.4.3 Loops

Similarly, loops can be executed by *make*. The restriction is that the loop must be placed all on one line [the use of a backslash (\) to continue a line is useful with loops]. For example (assuming *make* is using *sh* to execute the commands):

```
DIRS = liba libb libc
alllibs:
        for d in $DIRS ; \
        do ; \
            (cd $d ; make all) ; \
        done
```

For more information about loops and other programming of the shells, see Chapter 9.

## 5.5  **Other** *make* **Targets**

It is also possible to put targets into *make* which do not generate any new files. A common example of this is the **clean** entry, which by convention removes all files that can be regenerated. For example, the following fragment is the **clean** entry from the *watcher* **makefile:**

```
clean:
        rm -f a.out core watcher *.o y.tab.c y.tab.h\
        y.output Make.out
```

[Note the backslash (\) which allows a line to be continued.] Besides **clean,** another target often found in **makefile** is **install,** which will install the program being made on the system. If the program were obtained from a source which is not known secure, it is a wise idea to check the **makefile** before doing a *make install* as root.

By default, *make* prints each command before executing it. For commands such as *echo*, it is distracting to see the command. If only a single command should not be printed, the line should begin with an at sign (@). For example:

```
clean:
        @echo removing unnecessary files.
        rm -f *.o a.out core
```

would produce the following output:

```
removing unnecessary files.
rm -f *.o a.out core
```

On the other hand, if none of the commands should be printed, the directive **.SILENT** alone on a line or a -s on the command line should be used.

## 5.6   Configuration of Systems

When a program is destined to be used on more than one machine or operating system, or otherwise needs to be configured differently at different invocations, two major methods are useful. The first and probably most common method is to have a .h file with many **#define**s for constants which control compilation. For example, a mail system needs to know which mail transport agent to use (two common ones are *sendmail* and *delivermail*). This information could be in a file, say config.h, in the following manner:

```
#define SENDMAIL
/* #define DELIVERMAIL */
```

where the incorrect **#define** is commented out. The definitions are then used in the code to select appropriate sections (via **#ifdef**), depending on the particular mail transport agent. In this way, **config.h** is the only (hopefully!) source file which needs editing when bringing this mail system up on a new computer.

```
# Select the mail transfer agent for your site:
# MTA = DELIVERMAIL
MTA = SENDMAIL

# several more macro definitions for other configuration parameters

DEFINES = -D$(MTA)

CFLAGS = -O $(DEFINES)
```

**Figure 5.8**  Example showing configuration of systems with *make*.

On the other hand, in most cases when a new piece of software is being brought up, the **makefile** needs editing to reflect local preferences for new commands, library locations, or other differences from the system where the **makefile** was generated. The **makefile** could have macros defined for these configuration options as in Figure 5.8. The **makefile** builds the proper configuration #defines from the *make* macros.

*watcher* uses the **makefile** method for controlling configuration. Only one configuration parameter exists for *watcher*—the operating system type (Berkeley or System V).

## 5.7  Summary

*make* is used to ensure that all files in a system are up to date. To determine if a file is out of date, *make* looks at the time the file was last modified and the information about dependencies supplied in the **makefile.** If the file is out of date, commands to reconstruct it can be supplied in the **makefile,** or *make*'s implicit rules can be used. *make* has macros which allow common things such as compiler flags to be specified once for all invocations of the compiler.

Since learning by example is best, the **makefile** for *watcher* is presented in Appendix E.

# CHAPTER 6

# Writing and Debugging Revisited

## 6.1 Introduction

In Chapter 4 it was mentioned that the parser builds a structure which represents the control file, and the rest of the program determines the tasks to perform based on the information in this structure. At this point, writing the code that acts upon this structure is all that remains. Since this is primarily C programming, this chapter will cover only the points which relate to tool building. The complete code for *watcher* appears in Appendix E.

This chapter also contains hints on how to debug a tool both as it is being written and after it is finished (except, of course, for "that one last bug"). These hints include using *lint* and the debuggers supplied with the system (such as *dbx* or *sdb*).

## 6.2 Building a Structure with *yacc*

The first step in design is to determine how we will represent the control file in a data structure for the rest of the program to use. Next, we will debug the parser by writing a collection of routines to pretty-print this structure (pretty-printing as a debugging aid was discussed in Section 2.6).

The structure built by *watcher*'s parser consists of three parts:

1. The command to execute
2. The output format describing how to parse the output of the command
3. The description of what is normal, detailing how the output may change and still be considered normal

Each of these parts is a linked list. A graphical depiction of the structure which the parser builds is in Figure 6.1; each of the items in a bubble is a structure (defined in **defs.h**). A command consists of the following parts:

pipeline   To execute

alias   For the command (if any)

key   A pointer to an output format structure which describes how to find that part of the line to be used as a key; keys are used to match lines of output between runs of *watcher*

output format   A pointer to a list of all of the items which appeared in the output format

description of normal   A pointer to a list of change formats describing what is considered normal for this command

The output format and change format structures contain fields for each of the items which appear in the parser description. For example, the *watcher* control file (Figure 6.2) will be represented by the structure in Figure 6.3.

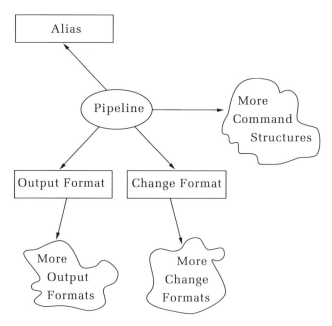

**Figure 6.1**   Structure built by the *watcher* parser.

```
(ps -aux |tail +2 |fgrep -v -f Daemons)
{'ps with no daemons'}
        9-14 pid%k 42-45 cputime%d:
            cputime 0 10.

(uptime |sed 's/.*://' |sed 's/,//g')
{'local load average'}
        1 load %d:
            load 0 10.

(df -i |tail +2) { df }
        1 filesystem%k 5 spaceused%d 8 iused%d:
            spaceused 15%;
            spaceused 0 89;
            iused 10;
            iused 0 75.
```

**Figure 6.2**   Sample *watcher* control file.

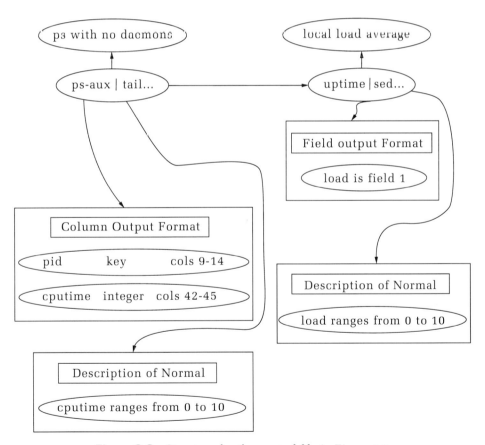

**Figure 6.3**   Structure for the control file in Figure 6.2.

Given this description of the structure built by the parser, it is fairly easy to produce a collection of routines capable of producing a pretty-printed version of the control file. Appearing in Appendix E, they are **pp.c**, **pp_out.c**, and **pp_change.c**. As mentioned in Section 2.6, we will use pretty-printing of the control file to aid in debugging the parser. The pretty-printing feature will also help when the parser is enhanced in the future by allowing the parser to be tested first, and once it is known to be functioning properly, the rest of the code will be added and tested. A version of the main program which only does pretty-printing is presented in Figure 6.4.

For further testing of the parser, we can create a control file which exercises most of the code in the parser (Figure 6.5). Since much of the parser is devoted to building linked lists, the test control file needs to check both when there is one item in a list and when there are multiple items (at least three). This testing will ensure that lists are built properly.

```
/*
main: main routine for the watcher program which does nothing but
pretty-print.

Kenneth Ingham

Copyright (C) 1987 The University of New Mexico
*/

#include "defs.h"

main()
{
        extern int parse_error;
        extern struct cmd_st *clist;

        if (yyparse() == 1 pipepipe parse_error) {
            fprintf(stderr, "%s: parse error in control file.\n", NAME);
            exit(1);
        }

        if (clist == NULL) {
            fprintf(stderr, "No command list to execute!\n");
            exit(1);
        }
}
```

**Figure 6.4**   **main** for *watcher* which only does pretty-printing.

```
# Watcherfile to test most of watcher's parsing and change formats.
#

# col out fmt with a one col entry
# float values
( ruptime )
        1 host %k 2 status%s 7 load1 %f 8 load2%f 9 load3 % f:
                status "up";
                load1 0.0 0.5;
                load2 1.3%;
                load3 .01.

# field output format
# string change format
# comment in entry
(rwho pipe grep a)
        1 user %s 2 tty %s 3 month %s:
                        user "ingham", "datkins", "cs2532ao", "cs5371ad";
                month "Oct".

# field output format with only one item
# max min change format
# only one change format
# alias
(rwho) { 'rwho 1' }
        4 date %d:
                date 1 8.

# col output format
# absolute change format
# percent change format
# integer values
(rwho) { 'rwho 2' }
        1-25 user_and_tty %k 27-29 month % s 31 - 32 day%d
        34-35 hour %d 37-38 minute %d 41-42 idle %d:
                day 1 7;
                minute 2%;
                idle 2.
```

**Figure 6.5** Control file for *watcher* which tests features of the parser.

When the parser is not working correctly, the pretty-printer either fails (with a core dump) or prints an incorrect version of the control file. In either case, the output of the pretty-printer provides a good clue to the location of the problem.

It is worthwhile to note that the structure is not modified by any part of the program other than the parser. If changes occur (which can

be determined by placing a call to the pretty-printer at strategic locations in the code), a bug exists. Since the parser is built out of storage
returned by **malloc,** the bug is probably a pointer problem, such as
using a **free**d pointer or a pointer which has garbage in it.

## 6.3 Use of the Structure Built by the Parser

Each major part of the structure (the bubbles in Figure 6.1) corresponds to a specific routine in the rest of the program. For example,
the routine **doit** loops through the commands and calls **checkline** to
go through each of the change formats. **checkline** calls **check_item** to
verify that a particular item is normal. This one-to-one correspondence between the data structures and the subroutines makes writing
and debugging easier. Without this correspondence, the structure
would be difficult to deal with. When *watcher* runs, the following
things will happen:

1. Parse the control file
2. For each process specified in the structure (each of the commands in Figure 6.1), use **popen** to open a pipe to the pipeline
   specified in the structure
   (a) Parse a line of output from the process
   (b) Compare the output to the description of normal

Each of these items has a corresponding routine.

The routine **checkline** is passed a single line of output from a
command. For each description of normal on the list, it finds the corresponding output format and then the appropriate portion of the
line. It then passes the change format and the data to the routine
**check_item** which does the actual checking to make sure that everything is normal. Breaking the work into logical units makes both writing and debugging easier.

It is in this section of *watcher* that the verbose option comes in
handy to aid in debugging. The verbose option (which was designed
with debugging in mind) prints the command being executed and the
line read in. With this information you can compare what *watcher*
reads from the process to the description of normal provided in the
control file and determine if

- the parsing of the output of the command is functioning correctly
- the description of how to parse the line matches what is being
  found by *watcher*

## 6.4 General Debugging Hints

### 6.4.1 *lint*

Debugging is the most time-consuming part of programming. One debugging aid often overlooked is the program *lint*, which is a useful companion to the C compiler. *lint* takes most of the same arguments as the compiler does but does not produce any code. Instead, *lint* will point out problems which cause the program to dump core or be non-portable; such as

- types and number of arguments to functions
- if a function returns a value, it always returns a value
- functions whose values are not used
- unused variables
- uninitialized variables
- unreachable statements
- loops not entered at the top
- logical expressions which are constant

*lint* is also of use when working on code which may end up being moved to another machine. A program which is lint-free is less likely to be making use of operating system- or machine-dependent features of the language. *watcher* is clean as far as *lint* is concerned.

For example, the small program in Figure 6.6 has several errors in it. The function **a** is passed three uninitialized arguments but only references two of them when it is declared. The arguments are also

```
main( )
{
        int b, c;
        double d;

        a(b,c,d);
}

a(x, y)
int x;
float y;
{
        if (x == 3)
                return 6;
}
```

**Figure 6.6** Sample C program with no syntax errors but several problems.

```
% lint lsamp.c
lsamp.c:
lsamp.c(6): warning: d may be used before set
lsamp.c(6): warning: c may be used before set
lsamp.c(6): warning: b may be used before set
lsamp.c(11): warning: argument y unused in function a
lsamp.c(15): warning: function a has return(e); and
return;
a: variable # of args. lsamp.c(12) :: lsamp.c(6)
a, arg. 2 used inconsistently lsamp.c(12) :: lsamp.c(6)
a returns value which is always ignored
%
```

**Figure 6.7**   Result of running *lint* on the C program in Figure 6.6.

declared to be different types in **a** and **main. a** is a function but only occasionally returns a value, which is then ignored. *lint* flags these errors with the messages in Figure 6.7.

## 6.4.2   Debuggers

Also useful when debugging are the debuggers provided with UNIX, specifically *sdb* or *dbx*.[1] Debuggers are programs which sit "around" the program being worked on, allowing the user to interactively run the program, stop and examine variables or the stack, or trace the program step by step in order to look for bugs.

Specifically, if a program dumps core, a debugger can be used to get a stack trace. This stack trace shows the sequence of procedure calls (with their arguments) which led up to the statement causing the problem. Variables can be examined (even linked lists traversed) to compare the defective state of the program to its proper state. For example, the program in Figure 6.8 has a bug in the procedure **proc.** An example of running this program and then using the debugger is shown in Figure 6.9. Note that in this case, the problem could have been found simply by running *lint*, which would have noticed the mismatched arguments.

If a program is not functioning correctly, it can be debugged by running it to a critical point, stopping it, and then running one line at a time. This procedure allows variables to be watched and compared with their expected values, and it also allows the exact flow of

---

1. Another debugger is almost always provided with UNIX also—*adb*, notable not for its ease of use but for the fact that it can work on the kernel and can be used to patch anything. I've even seen binaries from other operating systems patched with *adb!*

```
main( )
{
        int a, b;

        proc(a, b);
}

proc(x, y)
int x, *y;
{
        *y = func(x); /* bug: y was not passed an address */
}

func(var)
int var;
{
        return 6 * var + 35;
}
```

**Figure 6.8**  Program which dumps core.

```
% cc -g dump.c
% a.out
Bus error (core dumped)
% dbx a.out
dbx version 2.0 of 5/2/89 0:29.
Type 'help' for help.
reading symbolic information ...
[using memory image in core]
(dbx) where
proc(x = 0, y = (nil)), line 11 in "dump.c"
main(0x1, 0x7fffdfe8, 0x7fffdff0), line 5 in "dump.c"
(dbx) stop in func
[1] stop in func
(dbx) run
[1] stopped in func at line 16
16 {
(dbx) step
stopped in func at line 17
17        return 6 * var + 35;
(dbx) step

Bus error in proc at line 11
11        *y = func(x); /* bug: y was not passed an
address */
(dbx) quit
%
```

**Figure 6.9**  Using a debugger with a program which dumped core.

the program to be seen. This combination allows the programmer to quickly locate the source of the problem. An example of this process is shown in Figure 6.9.

### 6.4.3 **printf** Statements

An alternative approach to using a debugger involves strategic placement of **printf** statements in the code, indicating when a program has reached a critical point and providing the values of critical variables. In the case of *watcher*, some of these are left in permanently, to be accessed by running in verbose mode. A disadvantage of **printf** statements is the time necessary to put them in the proper file, recompile, and then run the program—a debugger does the equivalent without the editing and compiling.

## 6.5  Summary

The parser builds a structure which the rest of the program uses. Once it is built, the program uses this structure to know what programs to run, what portion of the output is interesting, and how it can change without being classified as "abnormal."

Debugging is often the most time consuming part of programming. A number of options exist, however, to reduce debugging time. For *watcher*, pretty-printing is used as a debugging aid to verify that the structure is built correctly. The program *lint* is a valuable aid to debugging. It identifies several potential problems which can cause the program to fail or be nonportable. Debuggers provided with UNIX, *dbx* and *sdb*, are useful to identify the cause and location of core dumps, as well as tracing programs to find out where they are not functioning correctly.

Thought should be given as to what information will be useful when debugging the program later, as enhancements are added. This information should be made available with **printf** statements strategically placed in the code, which can be easily turned on.

# CHAPTER 7

# Writing Documentation

Getting the program running is only part of the task of writing a tool for UNIX. A program is not a tool unless others can use it to solve their own problems. Proper documentation is a necessity.

## 7.1  The Manual Page

UNIX has a standard for documentation—the manual page.[1] Provided as reference with all UNIX systems, and often available on-line via the *man* command, these documents provide a reference manual for the entire system. When writing a manual page it is important to provide all of the information that a person with a reasonable background with UNIX would need in order to use the new tool.

## 7.2  Standard Headings

There are several standard headings which are used in the manual pages.

NAME   The name of the command along with a one-line summary.

SYNTAX (also known as SYNOPSIS)   The syntax of the command, showing all arguments. The command is in boldface with optional arguments in brackets ([ and ]). Items which are filled in by the user (such as file names) are in normal (roman) type.

1.  This may be more than one page long.

DESCRIPTION A detailed description of how to use the command and what it does (including any control language), and a description of each of the arguments or flags. In this section, the command name and arguments are written in italics.

DIAGNOSTICS A description of any diagnostic messages or exit codes. This section is included only if a useful error status is returned or if some of the error messages need explaining.

BUGS (also known as RESTRICTIONS) A list and description of any shortcomings or restrictions in the program which may cause the user problems. Ordinary bugs should be fixed and not documented.

FILES A list of the full pathnames of all files which the program uses. This heading is useful when tracking down odd error messages. Seeing the files used may provide an insight as to the problem.

SEE ALSO A list of related or complementary commands.

Some vendors have changed the names slightly, and occasionally other headings are added (such as **REQUESTS,** which appears in the manual page for the macros for formatting manual pages). Not all commands need all of the headings, and finally, the order may differ depending on the vendor.


## 7.3   Macros for Formatting Manual Pages

The manual pages on UNIX are formatted with the *nroff* or *troff* text formatter and a special set of macros. A detailed description of *nroff* and *troff* are beyond the scope of this book. However, this chapter will give a quick overview of the macro package used for manual pages and how to use it. In this section, any references to *troff* also apply to *nroff* unless specifically noted.

The macros used when formatting a manual page are described in **man**(7). Many of these descriptions are not complete; if you look in the source for the manual pages, you will find macros used which are not described anywhere. All of the macros described in this section are described in **man**(7).

Like any piece of text, manual pages have a title and are broken into sections, subsections, and paragraphs. Table 7.1 summarizes the macros for each type of text unit. The *watcher* manual page in Appendixes B and C uses all except the subsection macro.

**Table 7.1**
Macros for Producing Headings in Manual Pages

| Command | Argument(s) | Notes |
|---------|-------------|-------|
| .TH | Name, chapter, extra-commentary[a] | Title and heading |
| .SH | Heading | Section heading |
| .SS | Heading | Subsection |
| .PP | Heading | Paragraph |

[a]Name is the name of the command, such as *watcher*. Chapter is the section of the manual: 1 for commands, 2 for system calls, etc. The extra-commentary is placed in the trailer of the manual page at the bottom.

If there are spaces in any of the arguments to the commands, the argument must be enclosed in quotation marks ("). For example, a heading command of the form

```
. SH SEE ALSO
```

will be printed like

**SEEALSO**

The solution is to enclose the string in quotation marks (") as in

```
. SH "SEE ALSO"
```

which will have the desired effect and produce

**SEE ALSO**

as output.

The commands in Table 7.2 change the font. The font commands may be followed by up to six words to be printed in the different font. For example:

```
. B bold
```

would produce the following line:

**bold**

If nothing follows the font command, the next line is written in the changed font. For example:

```
. B
this line will be bold
and this one will be roman
```

**Table 7.2**

Font Changing Commands in the Macros
for Manual Pages

| Command | Result |
| --- | --- |
| .B | Bold |
| .BI | Bold and italic alternating |
| .BR | Bold and roman alternating |
| .I | Italic |
| .IB | Italic and bold alternating |
| .IR | Italic and roman alternating |
| .RB | Roman and bold alternating |
| .RI | Roman and italic |

will produce the following output:

**This line will be bold**
and this one will be roman

If the macro is given an argument to make bold, the spaces between
the words are removed (the same as with the headings). If you want
spaces in the words, use quotation marks (") around the words.

```
.B run together " and separate"
```

produces

**runtogether and separate**

Also in Table 7.2 are several commands which alternate the font.
For example,

```
.BI
bold italic and more text
```

produces

**bold** *italic* **and** *more* **text**

These alternating font commands can be useful in the description of
the argument list (see the manual page for *watcher* for an example).
They are also used in the manual page for *csh* when describing the
syntax of the control flow. For more examples, go to the directory con-

```
.TH extabs 1 Local ¨
.SH NAME ¨
extabs - expand tabs ¨
.SH SYNTAX ¨
.B extabs ¨
[ file ...] ¨
.SH DESCRIPTION ¨
.I extabs ¨
expands tabs to spaces. It reads from the standard input or from the ¨
files listed as arguments. ¨
.PP ¨
.I extabs ¨
assumes that tab stops are every eight spaces. ¨
.SH "SEE ALSO" ¨
expand(1) ¨
.SH BUGS ¨
Should be able to specify tab stops somehow. ¨
.SH AUTHOR ¨
Kenneth Ingham ¨
.br ¨
The University of New Mexico ¨
```

**Figure 7.1**  Unformatted manual page for *extabs*, the tab expander.

taining the manual pages (**/usr/man/man1** is a good place to start) and *grep* for the *nroff* commands you are interested in seeing.

A few other *troff* commands should be mentioned. Comments are started by \" and continue to the end of the line. To cause a line break, a **.br** is used. **.ad** causes the paragraphs to be adjusted and filled, so that the text always ends at the same column on the line.

In Figure 7.1 is an unformatted manual page for *extabs* which was developed in Section 3.5.4. The manual page is formatted in Figure 7.2.

As another example of how to write manual pages, formatted and unformatted versions of the manual page for *watcher* are provided in Appendixes B and C. Additional examples may be found by looking at the manual for the system and looking at the unformatted manual pages stored in /usr/man/man?/* on many systems.

## 7.4  Formatting the Manual Pages

While the *man* command formats the manuals for you, it is useful to know how to produce manual pages manually. As mentioned earlier,

extabs(1)                   UNIX Programmer's Manual                   extabs(1)

**NAME**
    extabs - expand tabs

**SYNTAX**
    **extabs** [ file ...]

**DESCRIPTION**
    *extabs* expands tabs to spaces. It reads from
    the standard input or from the files listed as
    arguments.

    *extabs* assumes that tab stops are every eight
    spaces.

**SEE ALSO**
    expand(1)

**BUGS**
    Should be able to specify tab stops somehow.

**AUTHOR**
    Kenneth Ingham
    The University of New Mexico

Printed 8/6/89                        Local                                1

**Figure 7.2**  Formatted manual page for *extabs*, the tab expander.

*troff* or *nroff* do the formatting with a special set of macros. The command used is

troff -man *file*

where *file* is the file to be formatted.

## 7.5   What Should Be Covered in a Manual Page

While all the topics that *should* be covered in the manual pages are often not, each of the following should be included in every manual page written:

- A list of all arguments and an explanation of what they do
- A description of all user-supplied arguments (such as filenames)
- An explanation of what the command does

- Examples of how to use the command
- All files which are used and not explicitly specified by the user
- Any command language used by the program (it should be both listed and explained)
- An explanation of the exit status if it means something (for example, see the manual page for *diff*)
- Any assumptions made by the program
- What the error messages mean
- References to related commands (via the **SEE ALSO** section)
- Limitations, bugs, or design shortcomings

## 7.6  Additional Documentation

If the tool is complex, an additional background paper is usually written which has a tutorial or overview emphasis. Examples of these papers include the papers on *yacc* by Johnson and on *lex* by Lesk which were referred to previously. These papers provide examples showing how to use the particular tool, and they provide information enabling an unfamiliar user to (with some playing with small samples) learn the tool and become proficient with it.

*watcher* is not as complex as *yacc*. Additional documentation explaining *watcher* exists in the form of a paper which was presented at the Summer 1987 Usenix Conference. This paper (see Appendix D) describes the background leading up to *watcher*, how *watcher* works, and how it is used at the University of New Mexico.

## 7.7  Summary

Every program should provide documentation. On UNIX, the standard of documentation is the manual page. Manual pages have several standard headings and several topics which should be covered. They are formatted with a special set of macros for *troff* or *nroff*, text formatters which are provided with UNIX.

Some larger programs are backed up by detailed supplementary documentation, explaining in yet further detail how they are used. These additional papers may be tutorial in nature or provide more detail about the theory behind the program.

# CHAPTER 8

# Useful Standard UNIX Tools

So far, this book has covered the tools which played an instrumental part in the building of *watcher*. This chapter will cover some of the tools which are used both in control files as part of the pipelines as well as during the everyday programming and other work for which people use UNIX. For more detail on any of the commands covered in this chapter, see Section 1 of Volume 1 of *The UNIX Programmer's Manual* (Appendix A contains hints which may help when reading the manual).

As an example, if the number of arguments to a routine is changed, it is useful to be able to change all of the places where it is called. This can be done easily with the following command:

```
% vi `egrep 'pp_main(' *.c`
```

which invokes the editor *vi* on all of the files which have a call to the routine **pp_main** (*egrep* will be covered in more detail in Section 8.2; the quoting used is covered in Section 9.3).

### 8.1 *head* **and** *tail*

These two programs provide a way of getting the first or last portion of something (by default 10 lines). For pipelines, *tail* is useful for removing headings (which are the first few lines) with a command such as

```
command | tail +2
```

which starts at the second line in the output of the command. A +n with *tail* means to take from the nth line through the end, while a

−n tells *tail* to only display the last *n* lines. For example, the output of *ps* is

```
PID     TT  STAT  TIME   COMMAND
12117  p0   I     0:07   -csh (csh)
12136  p0   I     0:40   lsh
12798  p0   S     0:06   /usr/ucb/vi chapter8.tex
12800  p0   S     0:02   sh -c ps
12812  p0   R     0:00   ps
```

When *ps* is piped to *tail +2*, the result is

```
12117  p0   I     0:07   -csh (csh)
12136  p0   I     0:40   lsh
12798  p0   S     0:08   /usr/ucb/vi chapter8.tex
12814  p0   S     0:02   sh -c ps | tail +2
12826  p0   R     0:00   ps
12827  p0   S     0:00   tail
```

*head* takes an optional argument −n, where *n* is the number of lines to display. *head* is useful for looking at the first portion of a file to determine what the file contains.

*head* and *tail* are not provided with all UNIX systems. If your system doesn't have them, consider writing them. They can be quickly written with *sed*, which is described in Section 8.5.


## 8.2  The *grep* **Family**


When it comes to searching for patterns, UNIX provides a multitude of tools. Supplied with all systems are the *grep* family: *grep*, *egrep*, and *fgrep*. Other programs which combine features of some of the greps or provide newer algorithms are available from sources such as the Free Software Foundation.

In normal use, the greps print the line containing a match for the pattern supplied on the command line to **stdout.** The -v option causes *grep* (or *egrep* or *fgrep*) to print only those lines which do not match. Several other options are documented in the manual.

*grep* takes regular expressions similar to those used by *ed* or *ex*. For example, looking for the user ingham in the password file, one could

```
grep ingham /etc/passwd
```

and receive the following output:

```
ingham:x9/Oe6VaioXzk:5003:10:Kenneth Ingham,B66G,78045,2776751,:/u1/ingham:/bin/csh
```

*fgrep* can also take its patterns from a file. This is useful when looking for one of many items where the regular expression for grep or egrep would be too long or messy. For example, with a file of daemons containing

```
sendmail
update
cron
lpd
inetd
```

the pipeline

```
ps ax | fgrep -f daemons
```

would look through the list of processes running on the system and print out only the processes listed in the file daemon. An example of output from this command is

```
 143 ? I  6:33 /etc/update
 146 ? I  5.14 /etc/cron
 152 ? I  0:24 /etc/inetd
 169 ? IW 0:03 /usr/lib/lpd
9332 ? I  1:04 /usr/lib/sendmail -bd -q15m
```

*fgrep* cannot handle regular expressions, and the items in the file must be on separate lines.

A useful option to all of the commands in the grep family is -v, which has grep print out only the lines which do not match the pattern(s). An example provided by a *watcher* control file in which one does not want to look at the daemons in all cases is discussed in Section 10.1.

The -l option was given as an example in the beginning of this chapter. It causes grep (or egrep or fgrep) to list only the names of the files which have lines matching the specified pattern.

The -i option causes grep/fgrep/egrep to ignore the case of letters when making comparisons. It is useful when the case is unknown or mixed.

The -s option causes grep/fgrep/egrep to be completely silent in its work. The results of the search are available in the exit status:

0 A line was found which matched.

1 No lines were found which matched.

2 Problems were encountered, e.g., files which could not be opened.

## 8.3 sort **and** uniq

The purpose of sort is indicated by its name. By default, it sorts its input (read from stdin or files) in ascending order. Flags are available to reverse the sort, sort numerically, and control which part of the input will be used for sorting. As an example of the usefulness of sort, to find the top processes by CPU minute on the system, the following pipeline could be used:

```
ps -ax | sort +3rn | head
```

This sends the output of ps to sort which sorts in reverse order (the r flag) numerically (the n flag) starting with the 4th column (note that the columns begin with 0, so 3 was specified on the command line). The output from this command is

```
  156 ?  S 289:29 /etc/rwhod
  170 ?  S 135:43 - -fd 75 0 -s 5 ttyv0 (Xqvsm)
  101 ?  S  16:49 /etc/biod 4
   99 ?  S  13:18 /etc/biod 4
  100 ?  S  12:55 /etc/biod 4
  102 ?  S  12:44 /etc/biod 4
  143 ?  I   6:34 /etc/update
  146 ?  I   5:14 /etc/cron
12494 pf I   3:07 (dclock)
12495 pf S   3:00 xload -geometry 120x84+780+0
```

Somewhat related to sort is the command uniq, which can be used to find and eliminate, or count, repeated lines. (It also has other functions which will not be covered in this book.) uniq needs the repeated lines to be next to each other in order to be noticed; sort can be used to accomplish this. An example of the usefulness of uniq is counting the number of invocations of each currently running process. The pipeline

```
ps ax | tail +2 | colrm 1 20 | sort | uniq -c | sort -rn
```

(*colrm* simply removes everything between the columns given to it as arguments; in this case it removes everything through column 20) produces a sorted list of all of the processes on the system and the number of invocations of each that are running, starting with the most common and working down to those that have only one. A sample output of this pipeline (edited a bit to allow it to fit on one page) is in Figure 8.1.

This example shows a UNIX peculiarity which bothers some people—no headings on the output to identify the various columns. Headings on output to be passed down a pipeline may confuse the next process. For example, a pipeline which counts the number of

```
32 (init)
28 -csh (csh)
11 /usr/etc/rlogind
 8 /etc/nfsd 8
 8 (biod)
 6 GB_daemon
 3 /usr/etc/telnetd
 3 -u (csh)
 2 rlogin hydra -l cs303av
 2 rlogin deimos -l fe120cg
 2 rlogin ariel -l cs303av
 2 mail
 2 /usr/etc/ftpd
 2 /etc/ypbind
 1 w
 1 vi p1.f
 1 vi hamiltonian.p
 1 vi dtime
 1 vi capture.p
 1 vi Warri.p
 1 vi Summer4.p
 1 vi Assign6.p
 1 uniq -c
 1 tail +2
 1 swapper
 1 sort
 1 ps ax
 1 colrm 1 20
 1 <defunct>
 1 /usr/lib/sendmail -bd -q1h
 1 /etc/update
 1 /etc/syslog
 1 /etc/inetd
 1 /etc/cron
 1 /etc/comsat
```

**Figure 8.1**  Output of ps ax | tail +2 | colrm 1 20 | sort | uniq -c | sort -rn.

processes on the system will be off by one unless the programmer re-members that *ps* places headings on its output. At one time, few UNIX programs had headings. With their increased occurrences, more pro-grams need to use *tail +2* to throw them away.

Headings can be placed on the output of a pipeline with the *sed* command. See Section 8.5 for information.

## **8.4**  *wc*

A simple but very useful program is *wc*, which counts lines, words, and characters. Given flags of –1 for lines, –w for words, and/or –c for characters, when combined with *grep*, *wc* can tell how many lines matched the pattern given to *grep*. For example,

```
ps -a | grep csh | wc -1
```

will tell how many instances of *csh* are running on the system at the moment. Sample output from this pipeline is

```
4
```

which is the number of *cshs* running on the system at this moment.

## **8.5**  *sed*

When transforming data, an editor is often useful. However, editors like *ex* can be slow when working on large files. They also cannot be used in the middle of a pipeline. The editor *sed* (Stream *ED*itor) ex-cells in both areas. It can use regular expressions, like *ed* or *ex*, in commands describing how to transform its input. It can also use com-plex scripts containing these commands (a solution to the Towers of Hanoi problem[1] written in *sed* was posted on USENET several years ago).

---

1. Legend has it that in Hanoi some monks were given 64 golden disks of decreasing size and three posts (labeled 1, 2, and 3). Initially, all of the disks were stacked in descending size on the post labeled 1. Their task is to move this stack of disks to the post labeled 3. In doing so, they can move only one disk at a time and at no time may a larger disk be above a smaller disk. When they finish moving the disks, the world is to come to an end. The solution to this problem lends itself well to recursion, and it is often used as an introduction to recursion in programming courses.

For example, when describing *uniq* earlier, the command *colrm* was used; *sed* also works:

```
ps ax | sed 's/.*:[0-9][0-9]//' | sort | uniq -c
```

is another solution which uses *sed* to replace the sequence of characters up to a colon followed by two digits and a space with nothing (note that there is nothing between the second and third slash).

When discussing the *grep* family, `grep ingham /etc/passwd` was given as an example. *sed* can also be used:

```
sed -n /ingham/p /etc/passwd
```

The –n option tells *sed* not to print anything on stdout unless specifically requested to. In this case, it is only lines with the string `ingham` which will appear on stdout.

In Section 8.3, headings were mentioned. *sed* can be used to place them on a pipeline. Continuing the example from Section 8.3, we could put

```
| sed -f headings
```

where the file **headings** contained

```
0a\
num process\
```

The output (edited for brevity) would be

```
num process
32 (init)
28 -csh (csh)
11 /usr/etc/rlogind
```

The file which *sed* read tells *sed* to append after the 0th line (before the first line) in the input. Everything until a line consisting of a period ( . ) alone on a line is added. Note that the lines are ended with a backslash (\). Each new line is a new command for *sed* so the lines which are all part of one command (such as in this example) must be made into one logical line.

With *watcher*, the **Makefile** uses *sed* to make minor changes on the **Makefile** itself. In order to print a copy of all of the source (via *make print*), the **Makefile** has to know what the source files are. After work has been done on *watcher*, the list in the **Makefile** may be out-of-date. The entry Makefile in the **Makefile** uses *sed* to format the list of sources produced by *ls* so that it is in the proper form for *make*. The **Makefile** for *watcher* is in Appendix E.

## 8.6 *awk*

One of the most unique tools that UNIX provides is the *awk* programming language. *awk* is powerful and programs can be quickly written in it. An entire book is devoted to *awk*[2]; only some highlights of *awk* are covered here.

An *awk* program is a sequence of pattern-action pairs. As *awk* reads a line of input, it is matched against the patterns; if a match is found, the corresponding action is executed. Patterns or actions may be missing. If there is no pattern, every input line matches; if there is no action, *awk* prints the line which matched.

*awk* is somewhat similar to *lex*, which also has an input file composed of pattern-action pairs. Unlike *lex*, *awk*'s patterns are more than just regular expressions; it can also do numeric comparisons. In addition, *awk* is an interpreted language, whereas *lex*-generated programs are compiled.

*awk* was used as a solution to the problems later handled by *watcher* (see Section 2.3). *awk* did an excellent job. However, work was needed to write a new *awk* program each time a new problem was discovered which was not handled by the current collection of programs. It was also difficult to watch for changes between runs.

### 8.6.1 Patterns

Patterns have many forms in *awk*. The simplest is a regular expression between slashes (/). All lines which match the regular expression have the associated action performed. For example, the pipeline: ruptime | awk '/^a.*/ {a++} END {print a}' counts the number of machines whose names begin with an a and prints that number on the standard output.

*awk* breaks a line up into fields. The first field can be referenced as $1, the second as $2, etc. $0 refers to the entire line. These field vari-

2. *The AWK Programming Language* by Alfred Aho, Brian Kernighan, and Peter Weinberger, Addison-Wesley, 1988.

ables can be used in expressions. For example, to look for machines whose load average is above 5, the following pipeline could be used:

```
ruptime | awk '$7 > 5'
```

Sample output of *ruptime* is shown in Figure 8.2. When this pipeline runs, it produces output like:

```
carina.unm.edu up 5+19:21, 9 users, load 8.42, 9.01, 9.10
```

Patterns do not need to be numeric comparisons. For example,

```
$3 == "watcher"
```

checks to see if the third field is the string watcher.

Patterns may be expressions and can be combined with AND (&&), OR (| |), or NOT (') to make compound expressions. Parentheses can be used for grouping. For example,

```
ruptime | awk '($1 == "ariel.unm.edu" || $1 == "carina.unm.edu") && $7 > 2'
```

checks the load average on only two machines. Sample output from this pipeline is

```
ariel.unm.edu  up 6+15:22, 20 users, load 2.27, 3.06, 3.10
carina.unm.edu up 5+19:23,  9 users, load 9.04, 9.00, 9.08
```

Two patterns do not match any input lines. Actions associated with the pattern **BEGIN** are executed before *awk* begins processing the input, which is useful for initialization. Actions associated with **END** are executed after all of the input has been read.

| | | | | |
|---|---|---|---|---|
| ariel.unm.edu | up | 6+15:22, | 20 users, | load 2.27, 3.06, 3.10 |
| avior.unm.edu | up | 1+06:54, | 0 users, | load 0.06, 0.00, 0.00 |
| biblio.unm.edu | up | 12+03:04, | 11 users, | load 0.71, 0.36, 0.31 |
| bilbo.unm.edu | up | 20+08:27, | 0 users, | load 0.00, 0.02, 0.03 |
| blackstone.unm.edu | up | 37+06:48, | 1 user, | load 0.27, 0.19, 0.16 |
| borris.unm.edu | up | 1+07:28, | 0 users, | load 1.32, 0.96, 0.53 |
| bullwinkle.unm.edu | up | 38+05:47, | 1 user, | load 3.57, 4.14, 2.94 |
| carina.unm.edu | up | +19:23, | 9 users, | load 9.04, 9.00, 9.08 |
| chama.unm.edu | up | 2+16:03, | 0 users, | load 0.38, 0.27, 0.02 |
| chimayo.unm.edu | up | 6+01:44, | 0 users, | load 0.16, 0.13, 0.14 |

**Figure 8.2** Sample output from *ruptime*.

One use of the **BEGIN** pattern is to change the way that *awk* breaks up lines. By default, fields are separated by blanks or tabs. If you wanted to work with the password file, this would not work well since the password file uses colons (:) to separate the fields. Therefore, the following pattern-action could be used to change the field separator to a colon:

```
BEGIN { FS = ":" }
```

which sets the value of the variable FS—*awk*'s regular expression describing where to break a line—to a colon. For example, the following *awk* program prints lines from the password file which have a uid less than 100:

```
BEGIN { FS = ":" }
$3 < 100
```

No action is needed with the pattern $3 < 100 since the action is to print the line—the default action. Output from this *awk* program might be

```
root:dWrM/Chfr.kMg:0:1:Mr System:/:/bin/csh
field:U2XUOVeJmWjfc:0:1:Field Service:/usr/field:/bin/csh
nobody:Nologin:-2:-2:anonymous NFS user:/:
operator:PASSWORD HERE:0:28:the \$:/opr:/opr/opser
daemon:*:1:1:Mr Background:/:
sys:PASSWORD HERE:2:3:Mr Kernel:/usr/sys:
bin:PASSWORD HERE:3:4:Mr Binary:/bin:
```

## 8.6.2 Actions

An action is not required—if a pattern has no action, the lines which match are printed. When an action is supplied, it consists of statements (which are similar to C statements) enclosed in braces. The opening brace must be on the same line as the pattern, but after that, the action may take as many lines as necessary. If more than one statement is put on a line, they must be separated by a semicolon (;).

The simplest action is to print all or part of the line which matched the pattern. For example, the action

```
{ print $1, "and also", $3 }
```

prints the first and third fields with two words of text between them.

The *awk* program

```
BEGIN          { FS = ":" }
$3 < 4         { print $1, "has uid", $3 }
```

produces the output

```
root has uid 0
field has uid 0
nobody has uid -2
operator has uid 0
daemon has uid 1
sys has uid 2
bin has uid 3
```

*awk* programs can be either in a file or on the command line. To invoke it with a program on the command line

awk 'prog' [input files]

Note that the program is enclosed in ticks to prevent it from being interpreted by the shell in any way; many *awk* programs contain characters which are special to the shell. The *input files* are optional. If they are not provided, *awk* reads from the standard input. To specify a file containing a program

awk -f *progfile* [input files]

where *progfile* is the name of the file containing the program.

### 8.6.3  Examples

In addition to the examples given here, several are provided in the manual page for *awk*; *The AWK Programming Language* by Aho, Kernighan, and Weinberger; and *Awk—A Pattern Scanning and Processing Language* also by Aho, Kernighan, and Weinberger.

An *awk* program to print the average size of the disk partitions mounted is

```
BEGIN          { sum = 0 }
               { sum += $2 }
END            { print "average size: ", sum / NR }
```

Note the use of the variable **NR** which is the number of records (lines)

which *awk* has seen so far. If the program is put into the file **average.awk,** the pipeline

```
df | tail +3 | awk -f average.awk
```

would produce

```
average size: 198232
```

when the output from *df* is as in Figure 8.3.

A variable related to **NR** is **NF,** the number of fields on a line. On Berkeley-based UNIX systems, the command *rwho* places the idle time for a user as the sixth field of its output. If there is no idle time, there are only five fields. To print a list of users who are idle, the following pipeline could be used:

```
rwho | awk 'NF > 5'
```

Sample output from this pipeline is in Figure 8.4.

*awk* can be used to keep totals. Suppose a file contained a list of users and the number of minutes of connect time (Figure 8.5). At regular intervals, additional data is added to the file. The file is sorted so

| Filesystem node | Total kbytes | kbytes used | kbytes free | % used | Mounted on |
|---|---|---|---|---|---|
| /dev/rz0a | 15343 | 8465 | 5344 | 61% | / |
| /dev/rz0g | 227079 | 8060 | 196312 | 4% | /Xstuff |
| fornax.unm.edu:/usr | 227079 | 152410 | 51962 | 75% | /usr |
| fornax.unm.edu:/vars/var.corona | 61423 | 45406 | 9875 | 82% | /usr/var |
| hydra.unm.edu:/usr/spool/mail | 112197 | 76994 | 23983 | 76% | /usr/spool |
| fornax.unm.edu:/usr/spool/rwho | 227079 | 152410 | 51962 | 75% | /usr/spool |
| hydra.unm.edu:/p1 | 161627 | 126277 | 19187 | 87% | /p1 |
| carina.unm.edu:/p2/p2 | 201919 | 162972 | 18756 | 90% | /p2/p2 |
| avior.unm.edu:/p3/p3 | 227079 | 120781 | 83591 | 59% | /p3/p3 |
| nunki.unm.edu:/p4/p4 | 227079 | 122266 | 82106 | 60% | /p4/p4 |
| hydra.unm.edu:/u1 | 104491 | 70458 | 23583 | 75% | /u1 |
| hydra.unm.edu:/u2 | 104491 | 86898 | 7143 | 92% | /u2 |
| hydra.unm.edu:/u3 | 169635 | 150084 | 2587 | 98% | /u3 |
| hydra.unm.edu:/u7 | 112197 | 92418 | 8559 | 92% | /u7 |
| hydra.unm.edu:/u10 | 169635 | 124763 | 27908 | 82% | /u10 |
| hydra.unm.edu:/u11 | 161627 | 134813 | 10651 | 93% | /u11 |
| carina.unm.edu:/u12 | 404127 | 138274 | 225441 | 38% | /u12 |
| carina.unm.edu:/u14 | 265575 | 49023 | 189995 | 21% | /u14 |
| carina.unm.edu:/b1 | 586718 | 247937 | 280110 | 47% | /b1 |

**Figure 8.3** Sample output of *df*.

```
cs2531as   carina.unm.edu:ttyq9       Nov 19 19:43 :  04
donna      nukem.unm.edu:ttyp0        Nov 19 13:20 :  44
ee337ab    merlin.unm.edu:ttyp3       Nov 19 18:47 :  01
gshore     sevilletta.unm.edu:tty02   Nov 19 11:34 :  28
jsmith     biblio.unm.edu:tty00       Nov 19 18:05 :  08
ksalari    ariel:ttyp1                Nov 19 19:12 :  19
me3141ae   hydra.unm.edu:ttypV        Nov 19 19:36 :  12
mnutter    hydra.unm.edu:ttyp3        Nov 19 19:59 :  01
oper       ariel:ttyT4                Nov 19 19:02 :  25
rasure     peabody.unm.edu:ttyv0      Nov 19 13:45 :  01
shawver    hydra.unm.edu:ttyp4        Nov 19 14:38 :  06
stump      vaxell.unm.edu:ttyv0       Oct 28 13:26 :  50
```

**Figure 8.4** Output from the pipeline rwho | awk 'NF > 5'.

```
armstng 12
becky 53
cmorrow 56
collier 16
ctroup 52
datkins 46
donna 17
edward 24
emullins 06
eric 32
ingham 02
jlessard 33
```

**Figure 8.5** Original user data.

that lines with the same username are next to each other (Figure 8.6)
the program in Figure 8.7 will condense the file (Figure 8.8).

This example also shows **if** statements in *awk*. The syntax of the **if**
statement is

if ( *expression* ) *statement* else *statement*

where the **else** and the corresponding *statement* is optional. If you
want to have more than one statement, they must be surrounded by
braces (as in the C language). expressions are similar to those in C.

*awk* also has loops. The syntax for **for** and **while** loops is identical
to the C **for** and **while** loop syntax.

A final example is an *awk* program which was used to reformat
data destined for an IBM program at the University of New Mexico.
The input is several lines of accounting data, one line for each type of
charge and user. The output is a single line which has all of the user's

```
armstng 12
armstng 16
becky 10
becky 53
cmorrow 56
cmorrow 8
collier 12
collier 16
ctroup 14
ctroup 52
datkins 10
datkins 46
donna 13
donna 17
edward 14
edward 24
emullins 06
emullins 19
eric 10
eric 32
ingham 19
ingham 2
jlessard 17
jlessard 33
```

**Figure 8.6**   Data file with more data added.

```
        {
                if (NR == 1) {
                        previous = $1
                        sum = $2
                }
                else if (previous == $1)
                        sum += $2
                else {
                        print previous, sum
                        previous = $1
                        sum = $2
                }
        }
END     {
                if (NR > 0)
                        print previous, sum
        }
```

**Figure 8.7**   *awk* program to join two data files.

```
armstng 28
becky 63
cmorrow 64
collier 28
ctroup 66
datkins 56
donna 30
edward 38
emullins 25
eric 42
ingham 21
jlessard 50
```

**Figure 8.8**   Data file after *awk* runs with the program in Figure 8.7.

```
C10002    UNIX   UNMA882730408068826911ON0000708
C10002    UNIX   UNMA8827304080688269112N0000100
C10002    UNIX   UNMA8827304080688269113N0000061
C10002    UNIX   UNMA8827304080688269114N0000021
C10002    UNIX   UNMA8827304080688269118N0000021
C10002    UNIX   UNMA8827304080688269119N0000030
C10002    UNIX   UNMA8827304080688269120N0000015
C10003    UNIX   UNMA8827304080688269120N0000405
C10003    UNIX   UNMA8827304080688269128N0001797
C10016    UNIX   UNMA882730408068826911ON0012547
C10016    UNIX   UNMA8827304080688269111N0008600
C10016    UNIX   UNMA8827304080688269112N0000100
C10016    UNIX   UNMA8827304080688269113N0000586
C10016    UNIX   UNMA8827304080688269114N0001135
C10016    UNIX   UNMA8827304080688269118N0000025
C10016    UNIX   UNMA8827304080688269119N0000300
```

**Figure 8.9**   Sample input for the *awk* program in Figure 8.10.

charges on one line. Some of the input is in Figure 8.9, the *awk* program used is in Figure 8.10, and some of the output is shown in Figure 8.11. The idea behind this program is to collect the information in variables until the account number changes; then we print the information out and start on the next record.

This example uses the built-in function **substr,** a function which is given a string, the starting position, and the number of characters wanted (to the end of the string if this parameter is left out) and returns the portion of the string desired. There are several other built-in functions documented in the manual page for *awk* and *The AWK Programming Language* by Aho, Kernighan, and Weinberger.

```
BEGIN              {
            disk = 0;
            cpu = 0;
            printer = 0;
            mag_tape = 0;
            connect = 0;
            prev = "";
            machine = "";
            date = "";
        }


        {
#           print "Current", $1, "Prev", prev
            if (NR > 1 && $1 != prev) {
                printf "%s %s %s %7d %7d %7d %7d %7d\n", \
                    substr(prev,2),\
                    date, machine, connect, disk, printer,\
                    mag_tape, cpu;
                disk = 0;
                cpu = 0;
                printer = 0;
                mag_tape = 0;
                connect = 0;
                prev = "";
                machine = "";
                date = "";
            }

            type = substr($0,60,3);
            machine = substr($0,40,4);
            date = substr($0,44,5);
            amount = substr($0, 64, 7);

            if (type == "113" pipeline type == "118" pipeline type == "119")
                cpu += amount
            else if (type == "111")
                printer += amount
            else if (type == "110")
                disk += amount
            else if (type == "115")
                mag_tape += amount
            else if (type == "114" pipeline type == "120" pipeline type == "128")
                connect += amount
            else if (type == "112")
                flat_rate = amount # no-op - we don't use flatrate
            else {
                print "Unknown type", type, "Line: "
                print
            }
```

**Figure 8.10** *awk* program which transforms the data in Figure 8.9 to that in Figure 8.11. (*Figure continues.*)

```
        prev = $1
    }
END     {
        # print the last line...
        printf "%s %s %s %7d %7d %7d %7d %7d\n", \
            substr(prev,2),\
            date, machine, connect, disk, printer,\
            mag_tape, cpu;
    }
```

**Figure 8.10**  (*continued*)

```
10002 88273 UNMA     67     708      0  0    112
10003 88273 UNMA   7620   19486   1600  0   5056
10321 88273 UNMA   1891    1681  56315  0   2882
11322 88273 UNMA     11      48      0  0     70
11344 88273 UNMA     23    5533      0  0     42
12000 88273 UNMA    538    2675      0  0   1332
12177 88273 UNMA     68     103      0  0     33
12219 88273 UNMA    227     105      0  0    301
12233 88273 UNMA      0      38      0  0      0
12684 88273 UNMA      0      33      0  0      0
12685 88273 UNMA      0      15      0  0      0
12790 88273 UNMA     48     896   8100  0     17
```

**Figure 8.11**  Sample output from the *awk* program in Figure 8.10.

## 8.7  Summary

The tools covered in this chapter are useful both in everyday program-ming and in control files for *watcher*. *head* and *tail* show the first or last portion of a file or data coming down a pipeline. The commands in the grep family search for patterns. *sort* does the obvious and *uniq* works with repeated lines, counting or eliminating them. *wc* is good at counting words, lines, and characters. *sed* allows editing of data which either does not fit into an ordinary editor or is passing through a pipeline. Finally, *awk* is a programming language which is powerful and easy to use.

These tools are but a sampling of the tools provided with UNIX. For more information, see Section 1 of Volume 1 of *The UNIX Pro-grammer's Manual*.

# CHAPTER 9

# Programming the Shells

## 9.1  Overview

At this point, *watcher* is written and some of the standard UNIX tools which are useful in writing pipelines for control files have been discussed. However, no discussion of UNIX tools would be complete without covering the writing of shell scripts (which can also be tools).

Two shells (command interpreters) are available on almost all UNIX systems: *csh* and *sh*. Other shells may also be available but have limited distribution, therefore *csh* and *sh* will be discussed here.

Both shells are programming languages in their own rights. Writing a program in the shell often allows one to solve a problem more quickly than writing a program in a compiled programming language. For illustrations of this, look at any of the examples in this chapter.

The name "shell" refers to the fact that the command interpreter is the outer layer (or shell) of the operating system. In UNIX, as previously mentioned, the shells traditionally are also programming languages in their own right. They have variables and control flow. The statements rather than being computational in nature tend to be commands to execute. The shells can be programmed at the terminal by those who are accurate typists, and anything typed at the terminal can also be placed in a shell script.

The shells are described in more detail in their manual pages (**sh(1)** and **csh(1)**).

Shell scripts can be either placed in a file or typed directly at the terminal. If they are placed in a file, they can be run many times; if the script is complex, mistakes can be corrected easily. When typed at the terminal, the time needed to edit a file is avoided; however, accurate typing is a requirement, and to run the shell scripts again, they must be retyped.

When a shell script is placed in a file, chances are that the system will not recognize it as a shell script initially. The file must be made executable with the *chmod* command (e.g., chmod +x *file*).

Once the file is executable, it is run as any other command. Which shell will run it depends on which version of UNIX you are running. On System V Release 3 and earlier, the author knows of no good way. One solution is to use << (see Section 9.4 and Figure 9.2).

On Berkeley UNIX systems, if the first two characters of the file are #!, the command following these characters is run with the file as standard input for it. For example,

```
#! /bin/csh -f
echo hello world
```

would be run by */bin/csh* with the argument -f, no matter what the user's login shell is. All of the shell scripts given as examples use this method of identifying the shell to use.

When the shell processes a command, normally, it simply **fork**s and then **exec**s the command. Some commands (such as *cd*) may cause problems, especially in a loop. These problems can be avoided by executing the *cd* or other problem command in a separate shell. Commands placed within parentheses ( ( and ) ) are executed in a sub-shell. For example,

```
(cd source ; make all)
```

leaves the shell's current working directory alone, while still running the *make* in the subdirectory source.

## 9.2  Variables

### 9.2.1  Normal Variables

Both *csh* and *sh* have variables, which are stored as variable length strings (or arrays of strings). Variables are referenced by a $ followed by the variable name. Names are composed of upper and lower case letters, digits, or underscores. If the name is followed by a character which is not part of its name, such as a digit, other letters, etc., the name should be enclosed in braces ( { and } ). For example, in *csh* (*sh* is similar)

```
% echo $user
ingham
```

```
% echo $user.file
ingham.file
% echo $userfile
userfile: Undefined variable.
% echo ${user}file
inghamfile
```

Names do not have to be declared before use (actually, a syntax for declaring variables does not exist).

Variables may occur anywhere (but see Section 9.3).

Assignments are different between the shells. In *sh*, a variable is assigned a value (and created if it does not exist) by a line of the form

*name=value*

where *name* is the name of the variable and *value* is the string which is assigned to it. Note that there is no space around the =. For example:

```
var=abcdef
```

The string may contain other variables, as in

```
var=abcdef favorite_user=diana
```

With the above statements assigning variables, we can check their value with an *echo:*

```
$ echo $favorite_user
diana
$ echo $var
abcdef
```

(the *echo* can be used the same way in *csh*).

The special positional variables (which are described in Section 9.2.2) are assigned by the command **set.** For example:

```
set now is the time
```

sets $1 to now, $2 to is, etc.

In *csh* assignments are done via

```
set name = value
```

or

set *name* = ( *value value* . . . )

which creates an array which is referenced by $name [*index*]. If no subscript is given, the entire array is referenced.

### 9.2.2 Predefined Variables in *sh*

Both shells provide several predefined variables. In *sh*, they are

1 through 9   The arguments to the shell (positional variables). For example, $1 is the first argument, $2 the second, etc. $0 is set from argument 0 of the shell (usually the shell's name or the name of the shell script). They may be reset with the **set** command described above.

\#   The number of positional variables.

\*   All of the positional variables, as "$1 $2 . . . ".

@   All of the positional variables, as "$1" "$2". . . .

?   The exit status of the last command executed. This is useful for checking if a command failed or using a command like *grep* -s (silent) which reports its results via the exit status (the exit statuses are documented under the **DIAGNOSTICS** heading of the manual pages).

$   The process id of this shell.

!   The process id of the last background command executed.

### 9.2.3 Predefined Variables in *csh*

*csh* has more predefined variables. A few of them are

home   The home directory of the user who started the shell. This is set from the environment variable **HOME** (see below for more about environment variables).

path   An array with entries of all of the directories searched when a command is typed. It is initialized from the environment variable **PATH.**

status    The exit status of the last command.

cwd    The current working directory.

argv    The arguments to the shell. $*, $1, $2, etc. (like from *sh*) can be used and are synonyms for $argv, $argv[1], and $argv[2], respectively.

### 9.2.4  Environment Variables

In addition to the shell variables, another set of variables which are available to all programs are the environment variables (described in more detail in **environ**(7)). By default the following are set.

HOME    The home directory of the user running the program.

PATH    A list of directories to search for commands (the default path is limited and normally replaced with an expanded version).

USER    The login name of the user running the program.

SHELL    The login shell of the user.

Many programs change their behavior based on environment variables. For example, several programs such as the Berkeley mail program (*Mail* or *mailx* depending on the system), use the environment variable **EDITOR** when spawning an editor.

Additional environment variables can be set in *sh* by setting the variable normally and then using the command *export*. For example, to set a new path you could use

```
PATH=.:/bin:/usr/bin:/usr/local/bin:/usr/ucb
export PATH
```

The *export* command can take several variables to export to the environment at one time, such as

```
PATH=.:/bin:/usr/bin:/usr/local/bin:/usr/ucb
TERM=vt100
export PATH TERM
```

To set an environment variable in *csh*,

```
setenv name value
```

(note the lack of an =; it is not consistent with **set**). The PATH example from above done in *csh* would be

```
setenv PATH . : /bin: /usr/bin: /usr/local/bin: /usr/ucb
```

## 9.3  Quoting

There are times when a variable should not be replaced by its value. For example, in debugging, the statement

```
echo $variable has the value $variable
```

will produce the output (assuming **$variable** is set to **abcdef**)

```
abcdef has the value abcdef
```

simply printing the value of the variable `variable` twice with a few words of text in between. In order to avoid having variables (or other special shell characters like * and ?) expanded, they should be enclosed in ticks (' ). Redoing the above example, we get

```
echo '$variable' has the value $variable
```

which would echo

```
'$variable' has the value abcdef
```

Another way of quoting special characters to avoid their interpretation is the backslash (\). When it is placed before a special character, the character loses its special meaning. Yet another version of the example above is

```
echo \$variable has the value $variable
```

which would produce the output

```
$variable has the value abcdef
```

The other types of quotations expand variables but have other benefits. The quotation mark (") prevents the shell from breaking the quoted part into separate arguments. To make this more concrete, if the *printargs* shell script, given in Figure 9.14 or Figure 9.20, were invoked as

```
printargs "now is the time"
```

it would produce the output

```
argument 1 is 'now is the time'
```

but if it were invoked as

```
printargs now is the time
```

it would produce as output

```
argument 1 is 'now'
argument 2 is 'is'
argument 3 is 'the'
argument 4 is 'time'
```

Within quotes, variables and filenames (and in *csh*, history) are expanded normally. For example,

```
printargs "User is $USER"
```

would produce the output

```
argument 1 is 'User is ingham'
```

Another useful feature for shell scripts is the back-tick (or grave accent) (`` ` ``). A command placed within back-ticks is replaced by the stdout of the command with newlines changed to spaces. For example, in either shell

```
vi `grep -l fprintf *.c`
```

will invoke the editor *vi* on each of the files which contain a call (or other reference) of **fprintf.**

The different quote characters may be intermixed and used together; using all three at once

```
set fubar = " `echo $PATH | sed 's/:/ /g'`"
```

will set the array fubar to one element which is the path separated by spaces rather than colons. For example, if the variable **PATH** is set to

```
. : /u4/gnu/bin: /usr/ucb: /usr/bin/X11: /bin: /usr/bin:
```

then the variable **fubar** would have the value

```
. /u4/gnu/bin /usr/ucb /usr/bin/X11 /bin /usr/bin
```

## 9.4  Redirecting Input with $<<$

In both shells, the standard input may be redirected to come from a file with a $<$. However, another method of redirecting input exists but is used less frequently. Sometimes in a shell (*csh* or *sh*) script, a program gets more or less the same input each time the script is executed. This input can be provided with a redirection feature of the shells. When the shell sees the

*command* $<<$ *word*

it reads its standard input (which is usually the file containing the shell script, but this could also be typed at the terminal) until it comes to a line containing *word*.

For example, recently at the University of New Mexico, we needed to transfer some data to an IBM computer running MVS. The data had to be surrounded by JCL. The script which was used is in Figure 9.1. Note that within the JCL, variables appear which modify the JCL actually sent to the IBM. This script also illustrates several of the other concepts presented so far. In this script, on line 30 (the line which starts with //SYSUT2), the variables would be replaced with the values which were determined in lines 14–21 (the lines which begin with **set**).

If *word* is quoted in any way, the input does not have variables and filenames expanded. In the example in Figure 9.1, the input needed to have filenames substituted into the input so *word* was not quoted.

Figure 9.2 has an example in a shell script where *word* is quoted and the input is not expanded, even though it has variables in it. The command *at* created this file which would be executed at a time specified in the future (see the manual page for *at* for more information on how to use it).

```
#! /bin/csh -f
# senddata - send accounting data to the IBM. arguments tell us what the
# data is so we know where to put it once it gets to the IBM.
#
# read the actual data from stdin.
#
# usage: senddata dataname

if ($#argv != 1) then
        echo usage: senddata dataname
        exit 1
endif

set dataname = 'echo $argv[1] pipe tr a-z A-Z'
set tmpfile = /temp/to.ibm$$
set fullhost = 'hostname'
set host = 'basename $fullhost .unm.edu pipe tr a-z A-Z'
set date = ( 'date' )
set month = 'echo $date[2] pipe tr a-z A-Z'
set day = $date[3]
set year = 'echo $date[6] pipe sed -e 's/19//''

cat > $tmpfile << END_OF_ JCL
//T92229 JOB (92229,PASSWD), 'USER NAME', CLASS=A
/*ROUTE PRINT UNMMVS.RMT18
//*MAIL=INGHAM
//STEP1 EXEC PGM=IEBGENER
//SYSPRINT DD DUMMY
//SYSIN DD DUMMY
//SYSUT2 DD DSN=T92229.${dataname}.${host}.${month}${day}${year},
//DISP=(NEW,CATLG),UNIT=UDISK,
//SPACE=(TRK,(10,10),RLSE),DCB=(RECFM=FB,LRECL=80,BLKSIZE=3200)

//SYSUT1 DD DATA,DLM='@@'
END_OF_ JCL

# now put the data in the file
cat >> $tmpfile

# and the ending JCL
cat >> $tmpfile << END_OF_TRAILER
@@
//
END_OF_TRAILER

# and we're done. send it off
mail snarje@bootes < $tmpfile

# clean up and we're done
rm -f $tmpfile
```

**Figure 9.1**  Shell script to send data to an IBM which illustrates the <<.

```
cd /u1/ingham/book
umask 22
HOME='/u1/ingham'
export HOME
SHELL='/bin/csh'
export SHELL
TERM='xterms'
export TERM
USER='ingham'
export USER
PATH='.:/u1/ingham/bin:/usr/ucb:/usr/local/bin:/bin:/etc:/usr/bin:/usr/new:'

export PATH
/bin/csh << 'xxFUNNYxx'
make
xxFUNNYxx
```

**Figure 9.2** Shell script created by *at* which illustrates the << redirection of standard input where *word* is quoted.

```
if list1
then
            list2
else
            list3
fi
```

**Figure 9.3** Syntax of the **if** statement in *sh*.

## 9.5 Control Flow

Both shells are programmable and have control flow like more conventional programming languages. The syntax of the control flow varies between the shells however.

In *sh*, all of the keywords (**if, then, for,** etc.) must be the first word on the line or follow a semicolon ( ; ).

### 9.5.1 if

In *sh*, an **if** statement has the form shown in Figure 9.3, where *list* is a pipeline or a list (one or more pipelines separated by a semicolon ( ; )[1]).

When the *sh* executes an **if** statement, the following happens: *list1* is executed; if the exit status is 0, *list2* is executed. If the exit status of *list1* was nonzero, *list3* is executed.

1. More separators for a list of pipelines exist but are not as commonly used. See **sh(1)** for more information.

```
if list 1
then
        list2
elif list3
        list4
then
        list5
else
        list6
fi
```

**Figure 9.4**   Syntax of a more complex **if** statement in *sh*.

```
if grep -s ingham /etc/passwd
then echo ingham has an account on this machine
else echo ingham has no account on this machine
fi
```

**Figure 9.5**   Example of the **if** statement in *sh*.

The **if** statement also can be a multiway branch. The syntax is shown in Figure 9.4. In this case, if the exit status of *list1* is nonzero, *list3* is executed and its exit status determines whether *list5* or *list6* is executed. As many **elif-then**s as desired may be used.

The **if** statement in Figure 9.5 will inform the user whether or not ingham has an entry in the password file. Another way of writing the **if** statement is all on one line:

```
if grep -s ingham  /etc/passwd; then echo yes; else echo no; fi
```

This is useful in places such as makefiles where all commands can be no longer than one line.[2]

*csh* has two forms of an **if** statement. However, before they are covered, the idea of an expression in *csh* will be discussed. Expressions in *csh* are similar to those in C. The following operators are available for use in expressions and have the same meaning as in C:

```
| | &&
| ^ &
== != =~ ! ~ <= >= < > << >>
+ - * / % ! ~
( )
```

2. The line may be long and extended by use of the backslash, but it is still only one line.

=~ and ! ~ are not from C. $a =~ $b is true when $a and $b match after being expanded like filenames. Similarly, $a ! ~ $b is true when $a does not match $b.

Additionally, expressions may be command executions within braces ({ and }) which are true if they succeed (return 0 as exit status) and false otherwise. Finally, an expression may be of the form

*-l name*

*name* is expanded and then tested according to *l* to see if

r   User has read permission for the file *name*.

w   User has write permission on the file *name*.

x   User has execute permission for the file *name*.

e   The file *name* exists.

o   User owns the file *name*.

z   The file *name* is zero length.

f   The file *name* is a plain file.

d   The file *name* is a directory.

If *name* does not exist or is inaccessible, then all of these return false.

The first form of the **if** in *csh* is used when only one command needs to be executed when the condition is true. The syntax is

**if** ( *expr* ) *cmd*

where *expr* is an expression and *cmd* is a command to be executed when the expression is true. *cmd* must be a simple command; it cannot be a pipeline or list of commands in parentheses.

The other form of an **if** statement in *csh* has the syntax shown in Figure 9.6, where *commands* is one or more commands or pipelines. Note that only one **endif** is needed no matter how may **else if**s occur.

For example, two versions of the example provided for *sh* are in Figure 9.7.

```
if ( expr ) then
        commands
else if ( expr ) then
        commands]
else
        commands]
endif
```

**Figure 9.6**  Syntax of the *csh* **if** statement.

```
#! /bin/csh -f
# csh script showing the two forms of the
# if statement.

grep -s ingham /etc/passwd
if ( $status == 0 ) echo ingham has an account

grep -s ingham /etc/passwd
if ( $status == 0 ) then
        echo ingham has an account
else
        echo ingham has no account
endif
```

**Figure 9.7**  Two examples of the **if** statement in *csh*.

### 9.5.2  **case** or **switch**

Both shells have a construction similar to the C **switch** statement. The syntax in *sh* is shown in Figure 9.8. The *patterns* are the same as the patterns used for filenames. *word* is the string (or variable) to be matched by the patterns. *list* is a list of commands or pipelines (like with **if**). Note that the commands are ended by a double semicolon. An example of the *case* statement is shown in Figure 9.9, which checks the exit status of the command *diff* on the two arguments handed to the shell script and reports whether or not the files differ (but provides no information as to how they differ). Notice the **if** statement at the beginning which checks to make sure that enough arguments have been supplied.

In *csh*, the syntax is closer to the C language, as illustrated in Figure 9.10, where *string* is the string to be matched by one of the *patterns* supplied after the **case** statement. The label **default** is not required; if it is not supplied and nothing matches, then nothing is executed. The **breaksw** is required unless you want the execution to continue after the next pattern (similar to the C **switch** statement).

```
case word in
        pattern [pattern ...] )
        list ;;
        .
        .
        .
esac
```

**Figure 9.8**  Syntax of the **case** statement in *sh*.

```
#! /bin/sh
# sh script illustrating the case statement
#
if test $# != 2
then echo "usage $0 file1 file2"; exit
fi

diff $1 $2 > /dev/null
case $? in
0)
        echo "no differences" ;;
1)
        echo "differences found" ;;
2)
        echo "diff had problems" ;;
*)
        echo "unknown exit status from diff" ;;
esac
```

**Figure 9.9**  Example of the **case** statement in *sh*.

```
switch ( string )
        case pattern:
                commands
                breaksw
                .
                .
                .
        default:
                commands
                breaksw
endsw
```

**Figure 9.10**  Syntax of the **switch** statement in *csh*.

```
#! /bin/csh -f
# script illustrating the switch statement
#
if ( $#argv != 2 ) then
        echo "usage $argv[0] file1 file2"
        exit
endif

diff $1 $2 > /dev/nul
switch ( $status )
case 0:
        echo "no differences"
        breaksw
case 1:
        echo "differences found"
        breaksw
case 2:
        echo "diff had problems"
        breaksw
case *:
        echo "unknown exit status from diff"
        breaksw
endsw
```

**Figure 9.11**   Example of the **switch** statement in *csh*.

*patterns* are matched with *string* the same way that filenames are expanded. The example from the *sh* case statement translated to *csh* is in Figure 9.11.

### 9.5.3   **for** or **foreach**

The syntax of a **for** in *sh* is illustrated in Figure 9.12, where the variable name is set to the *words* one at a time, or, if **in** *words* is omitted, the positional parameters ($1, $2, etc.) are used. For example, to echo the various words from the command *date*, the script in Figure 9.13 could be used. (Note the ticks are back-ticks (`) not normal ticks (')) Figure 9.14 has an example of a script which uses a **for** loop to print its arguments.

The *csh* form of the **for** loop is the **foreach**. The syntax is given in Figure 9.15, where *name* is set to each element in *wordlist* one at a time. *wordlist* may be an array, a filename to be expanded, or any other construction which contains at least one item. An example of the **foreach** loop is in Figure 9.16 which looks at each of the files in the directories specified (or the current directory if none are speci-

```
for name in words ...
do
list
done
```

**Figure 9.12**   Syntax of the **for** statement in *sh*.

```
for arg in 'date'
do
        echo $arg
done
```

**Figure 9.13**   Example of the *sh* **for** statement.

```
#! /bin/sh
# printargs: program which prints the arguments
# it is given.
#
i=1
for arg
do
        echo "argument $i is '$arg'"
        i='expr $i is + 1'
done
```

**Figure 9.14**   An *sh* script which prints its arguments.

```
foreach name ( wordlist )
        commands
end
```

**Figure 9.15**   Syntax of the **foreach** statement in *csh*.

```
#! /bin/csh -f
# script which uses a foreach loop to
# find shell scripts in the directories
# given as arguments
#
if ($#argv == 0) then
        set dirs = .
else
        set dirs = $argv
endif

foreach d ($dirs)
        foreach file (${dirs}/*)
                file $file | grep -s script
                if ($status == 0) echo "$file is a script"
        end
end
```

**Figure 9.16**   A *csh* script illustrating the use of **foreach**.

fied) and checks the output of *file* to see whether the file is a script or not. Note the use of the -*s* option to *grep* to keep it quiet. Whether or not *grep* found the string is reflected in its exit status which is available in the *csh* variable **status.**

### 9.5.4 **while**

In *sh*, the **while** loop has the syntax illustrated in Figure 9.17, where *list* is as described in the section on **if** statements. The **do** *list* is optional.

As an example, suppose a process writes a log file when it terminates. To wait until the log file has been written (assuming it happens in a short period of time), the script in Figure 9.18 could be used. The script waits until $file exists and has something in it before exiting the loop. After the loop, it calls *more* to display the file one screen at a time.

In *csh,* a **while** statement has the form shown in Figure 9.19, where *expr* and *commands* are as defined in the section on **if** statements. The loop executes as long as *expr* is true. As an example of the **while** loop, Figure 9.20 has a *csh* shell script which prints its arguments.

```
while list
do
            list
done
```

**Figure 9.17**   Syntax of the **while** statement in *sh*.

```
#! /bin/sh
# script which repeatedly runs a
# command until the exit status is 0
while test ! -s $1
do
        sleep 30
done
echo "done. "
```

**Figure 9.18**   An *sh* script illustrating the **while** statement.

```
while ( expr )
        commands
end
```

**Figure 9.19**   Syntax of the *csh* **while** statement.

```
#! /bin/csh -f
# printargs: program which prints the arguments it is given.
#
set i = 1
while ($i <= $#argv)
        echo argument $i is \'$argv[$i]\'
        @i = $i + 1
end
```

**Figure 9.20** *csh* script which prints its arguments.

**repeat** *count* cmd

**Figure 9.21** Syntax of the *csh* **repeat** statement.

### 9.5.5 **repeat**

*csh* also has another form of a loop—the **repeat** loop. The syntax is shown in Figure 9.21, where *count* is the number of times to execute *cmd*, which can only be a simple command as in the one line **if** statement.

For example,

repeat 6 who

will execute the command *who* six times.

## 9.6  Debugging Shell Scripts

When debugging shell scripts the shell provides some assistance. If the shell is invoked with a –v flag, for example

sh -v fubar

every line is echoed as it is read (after history substitution if *csh*). Variables and filenames are not expanded.

As an example, Figure 9.22 shows the output when the *printargs* script given in Figure 9.20 is run with the –v option.

More useful is the –x flag, which prints each line right before it is executed. Variables, filenames, and history (*csh* only) are all expanded before the line is printed. Arguments to commands may be verified by using the –x flag. Each execution in a loop is shown, as are the executed branches of **if** statements.

The result of running *printargs* with the –x option is shown in Figure 9.23.

```
% csh -v printargs.csh now is the time

set i = 1
while ( $i < = $#argv )
echo argument $i is \'$argv[$i]\'
argument 1 is 'now'
@ i = $i + 1
end
while ( $i < = $#argv )
echo argument $i is \'$argv[$i]\'
argument 2 is 'is'
@ i = $i + 1
end
while ( $i < = #argv )
echo argument $i is \'$argv[$i]\'
argument 3 is 'the'
@ i = $i + 1
end
while ( $i < = #argv )
echo argument $i is \'$argv[$i]\'
argument 4 is 'time'
@ i = $i + 1
end
while ( $i < = $#argv )
%
```

**Figure 9.22**  Example of running a shell script with the -v option.

```
% csh -x printargs.csh now is the time
set i = 1
while ( 1 < = 4 )
echo argument 1 is 'now'
@ i = 1 + 1
end
while ( 2 < = 4 )
echo argument 2 is 'is'
argument 2 is 'is'
@ i = 2 + 1
end
while ( 3 < = 4 )
echo argument 3 is 'the'
argument 3 is 'the'
@ i = 3 + 1
end
while ( 4 < = 4 )
echo argument 4 is 'time'
argument 4 is 'time'
@ i = 4 + 1
end
while ( 5 < = 4 )
%
```

**Figure 9.23**  Example of running a shell script with the -x option.

Finally, nothing can replace the usefulness of the *echo* command which echoes its arguments. It can be used for debugging in a similar fashion as the **printf** statement is used in C.

## 9.7 More Examples

Several shell scripts are usually distributed with UNIX. They can be found by looking in the directories pointed to by your path and using the command

```
file * | grep script
```

which will list all of the shell scripts in the current directory. Even better is to write a shell script which looks on the path and finds shell scripts. Figures 9.24 and 9.25 contain *csh* and *sh* scripts which do this. How the command *file* identifies shell scripts varies depending on the version of UNIX which is running. The easiest way to determine what string to search for is to write a shell script and then check the output of the command

```
file script
```

where *script* is a file known to be a shell script.

## 9.8 Summary

The shells provided with UNIX are also interpreted programming languages. The shell scripts can be written at the terminal interactively

```
#! /bin/csh -f
foreach dir ($path)
        file ${dir}/* pipe grep script pipe sed 's/:..*//'
end
```

**Figure 9.24**   *csh* shell script which finds shell scripts on the path.

```
#! /bin/sh
for dir in ('echo $PATH pipe sed 's/:/ /g')
        file ${dir}/* pipe grep script pipe sed 's/:..*//'
done
```

**Figure 9.25**   *sh* shell script which finds shell scripts on the path.

or placed in a file, debugged, and run many times. The shells have variables and a control flow like that found in many procedural languages.

Two options for the shells make debugging easier: the –v option shows each line before variables and filenames are expanded and the –x option shows the lines right before they are executed. Additionally, judicious use of **echo** statements may aid in debugging.

# C H A P T E R  10

# **Using** *watcher*

Now that *watcher* is written, it is time to consider how to use it. At the University of New Mexico, we use *watcher* for its original purpose—to watch the systems. Based on mail received, most of the other users of *watcher* are using it for this purpose also; one site uses *watcher* to watch for changes in data being collected.

## 10.1  Customizing a Control File

Since most of the use of *watcher* is system watching, all of the examples presented in this chapter will be for system management. These examples are based on the control file used at the University of New Mexico.

To watch for large changes in disk space and for filesystems which are 90% or more full:

```
(df -i |tail +2) { df }
       1 filesystem%k 5 spaceused%d 8 iused%d:
              spaceused 15%;
              spaceused 0 89;
              iused 10;
              iused 0 75.
```

For example, consider a problem in the following sample output of *df -i* (Figure 10.1). Note that three filesystems (/dev/zd0a, /dev/zd0h, and /dev/zd1h) have more than 90% of the space used. When *watcher* is run, it produces the report in Figure 10.2.

In order to watch for machines going up or down, the following fragment may be used:

```
(ruptime | fgrep -f UnmHosts) {ruptime}
   2 status %s | machine %k:
        status.
```

| Filesystem | kbytes | used | avail | capacity | iused | ifree | %iused | Mounted on |
|---|---|---|---|---|---|---|---|---|
| /dev/zd0a | 7721 | 6434 | 514 | 93% | 1041 | 2799 | 27% | / |
| /dev/zd3h | 161627 | 92060 | 53404 | 63% | 13764 | 33340 | 29% | /u11 |
| /dev/zd3g | 169635 | 93182 | 59489 | 61% | 13816 | 35336 | 28% | /u10 |
| /dev/zd1h | 161627 | 132973 | 12491 | 91% | 11663 | 35441 | 25% | /p1 |
| /dev/zd1g | 169635 | 18 | 152653 | 0% | 14 | 49138 | 0% | /u3 |
| /dev/zd1a | 7735 | 67 | 6894 | 1% | 18 | 3950 | 0% | /tmp |
| /dev/zd2h | 104491 | 69967 | 24074 | 74% | 6516 | 36492 | 15% | /u1 |
| /dev/zd2g | 112197 | 80235 | 20742 | 79% | 5706 | 41398 | 12% | /u7 |
| /dev/zd0h | 104491 | 86240 | 7801 | 92% | 8364 | 34644 | 19% | /u2 |
| /dev/zd0g | 112197 | 85074 | 15903 | 84% | 8382 | 38722 | 18% | /usr |
| carina:/b1 | 586718 | 256585 | 271462 | 49% | 0 | −1 | 0% | /b1 |
| carina:/p2/p2 | 201919 | 155324 | 26404 | 85% | 0 | −1 | 0% | /p2/p2 |

**Figure 10.1**   Output of *df* -*i*, which shows some problems.

df has a max/min value out of range:
/dev/zd0a 7721 6434 514 93% 1041 2799 27% /
where spaceused = 93.00; valid range 0.00 to 89.00.
---------
df has a max/min value out of range:
/dev/zd1h 161627 132973 12491 91% 11663 35441 25% /p1
where spaceused = 91.00; valid range 0.00 to 89.00.
---------
df has a max/min value out of range:
/dev/zd0h 104491 86240 7801 92% 8364 34644 19% /u2
where spaceused = 92.00; valid range 0.00 to 89.00.

**Figure 10.2**   The result of running *watcher* with the control file fragment given in text and the output from *df* -*i* in Figure 10.1.

where the file **UnmHosts** contains

> ariel
> carina
> charon
> deimos
> europa
> fornax

This control file fragment will report any machine going down or coming up, since any change in status is to be noted. However, only one message will be produced when a machine goes down. For example, with the output from the pipeline in Figure 10.3 where the machine charon just went down, *watcher* would produce the report in Figure 10.4.

| | | | | |
|---|---|---|---|---|
| ariel | up | 5:29, | 2 users, | load 0.31, 0.25, 0.27 |
| carina.unm.edu | up | 5:50, | 4 users, | load 1.70, 1.47, 1.31 |
| charon.unm.edu | down | 14:42 | | |
| deimos | up | 16+22:27, | 1 user, | load 0.02, 0.10, 0.11 |
| europa.unm.edu | up | 8:51, | 0 users, | load 0.17, 0.11, 0.10 |
| fornax.unm.edu | up | 6:03, | 0 users, | load 0.73, 0.75, 0.49 |

**Figure 10.3** Output of *ruptime*.

```
ruptime has a value which changed:
charon.unm.edu down 14:42
where status = 'down'; it was 'up'
```

**Figure 10.4** Output from *watcher* when a machine goes down.

In order to watch the load average, noting if it gets large, the following control file fragment is used:

```
(uptime |sed 's/ *·//'|sed 's/,//g')
{'local load average'}
        ⊥ load %d:
            load 0 10.
```

An example report from this control file entry is

```
local load average has a max/min value out of range:
11.16 10.97 10.83
where load = 11.16; valid range 0.00 to 10.00.
---------
```

In order to watch for processes taking up lots of CPU time (excluding daemons which may use a lot of CPU time over the time that the machine is up), use the following control file fragment:

```
(ps -aux |tail +2 |fgrep -v -f Daemons)
{'ps with no daemons'}
      9-14 pid%k 42-45 cputime%d:
            cputime 0 10.
```

The file **Daemons** contains

```
biod
cron
inetd
mountd
```

named
nfsd
routed
sendmail
statd
update
ypserv

When *watcher* catches a process running a long time, it reports

```
ps with no daemons has a max/min value out of range:
root    9618 65.0 0.5 218 114 pc R 843:08 (ftp)
where cputime = 843.00; valid range 0.00 to 10.00.
---------
```

# APPENDIX A

# Where to Find More Information

This book is only a beginning; you will need to get more information as you continue to work with UNIX. This appendix discusses many of the ways of getting more information.

## A.1 How to Find Things in the Manual

*Note:* Some vendors are changing the layout of the manual, so this section may not apply to all UNIX documentation.

### A.1.1 Sections of the Manual

The documentation that comes with UNIX is divided into two parts—Volume 1 and Volume 2. Volume 1 is further broken down into eight sections:

Commands   Syntax and a description of all of the commands (except system administration commands) that come with UNIX. If you know what command you want to use but are not sure exactly how to use it, the answer is in this section of the manual.

System Calls   Usage and a description of all of the system calls. System calls provide direct access to the operating system but also often require you to keep track of more than the library functions.

Library Functions   Routines to make system calls easier to use, math libraries, graphics packages, and any other functions which have been provided with the system are described here.

Special Files   This section covers devices, their names, how to use them, and how to configure them into a kernel.

File Formats   Syntax or structures for all of the important or common files such as *tar* files, **termcap,** or **terminfo,** are described.

Games   This section describes how to play games on the system.

Macro Packages and Conventions   This is more or less a "miscellaneous" section of the manual. The macro packages supplied with the system for use with *troff* are described. Also in this section is an ASCII chart, a description of the environment, a quick tour through the filesystem (noting where many things live), and more

System Management Utilities   Programs or information not needed by the average user but of interest to system managers are described here. Some of the topics covered are backup and restore of the filesystem, what to do when the system crashes, and file system maintenance.

## A.1.2   The SYNTAX in Section 1

It takes a bit of experience to read the UNIX manuals. In Section 1, the material under **SYNTAX** section heading describes the syntax of the command. The command and any flags are in boldface. Items that you fill in with your specific value are in ordinary text (or sometimes in italics; it depends on the vendor). Optional items are in brackets ([ and ]). For example, the **SYNTAX** section of the manual page for *awk* is

**awk** [ **-F**c ] [ prog ] [ file ] ...

which means that *awk* has one flag, **F,** which if it is used must be immediately followed by some character (which is described later on in the manual page; in this case "c" stands for the character used to separate fields). The manual page notes when describing "prog" that it may be either an *awk* program or "**-f** progfile"—a file containing an *awk* program. A program does not have to be specified; if none is provided, *awk* does nothing except copy the "file"(s) it is given (if any) to the standard output. Since the ellipses (". . .") are present there may be more than one "file" specified. (In this case, the ellipses should have been inside the brackets. However, this is how it appeared in the manual page.)

Sometimes the arguments for a command are all strung together, such as this **SYNTAX** entry from the *csh* manual page:

**csh** [ **-cefinstvVxX** ] [ arg ... ]

With the arguments specified in this manner, the selected flags may all be strung together after one "-". For example,

```
csh -vx
```

is the same as

```
csh -v -x
```

### A.1.3   The SYNTAX in Sections 2 and 3

Sections 2 and 3 have syntax specifications which if not understood can cause lots of problems. If a #include line is given, then in order to use the constants or data structures discussed you need to include this file.

The variable declarations are as they are declared in the system call or library function. This is not necessarily how they are declared in the calling program. For example, the **execve** manual page has a syntax section which says

```
execve(name, argv, envp)
char *name, *argv[], *envp[];
```

which means that, as far as the system call is concerned, **name** is a pointer to a character. Frequently in the calling program this will be an array of characters. It may also be a pointer to space which was allocated via a call to **malloc.** In either case, it is assumed that the string is terminated with a null character. The array **argv** or **envp** may be an array of pointers to characters or a two-dimensional array. Once again, all of the strings are null terminated.

In Sections 2 and 3, the **SYNOPSIS** section can be misleading to the uninitiated. For example, the manual page for **time** (in Section 2 of the manual for System V and in Section 3 on Berkeley systems) has the following synopsis:

```
long ctime(tloc)
long *tloc;
```

Note that **time** is expecting a pointer to a **long** where *it will place the time.* You must allocate the space, either by passing the address of a **long** such as

```
long seconds;
    .
    .
    .
time(&seconds);
    .
    .
    .
```

or by allocating the space via a call to **malloc.**

In Section 2, the **DIAGNOSTICS** section describes the reasons the system call can fail and the value that the external variable **errno** is given. **errno** is a useful variable, allowing the program to decide what course of action should be taken, depending on the reason for the error. A program fragment which uses **errno** in this manner and tries to open the file **fubar** is shown in Figure A.1. If the open fails because the file does not exist, then the program continues after printing a message. Otherwise, some other error must have occurred and a descriptive message is printed out by the library function **perror.** The format of a **perror** generated message is

*string: message*

where *string* is the string passed to **perror** and *message* is the message associated with that error. For example, the message associated with **ENOENT** is "No such file or directory." A complete list of the error messages and an explanation of what happened is provided in the manual page **intro**(2), usually the first manual page in Section 2.

Volume 2 of the manual contains supplementary documents. It is in this section that the *lex* and *yacc* papers can be found. The documents in this volume contain tutorial or background information. To learn more about how to use the utilities, these are the documents to read.

## A.2  Experimenting

One of the best ways of learning how to use UNIX and the tools provided with it is to sit at a terminal and experiment. Try some of the pipelines presented in this book. Look up the commands in the man-

```
extern int errno;
int fd;

fd = open("fubar", O_RDONLY);

if (fd < 0) {
        if (errno == ENOENT) {
                printf("I couldn't find the file fubar!\n");
                printf("Continuing without it.\n");
                return;
        }
        else { /* a fatal error */
                perror("fubar");
                exit(1);
        }
}
```

**Figure A.1**   C code fragment showing use of the external variable **errno.**

ual and compare the manual to the behavior of the commands. Try changing them some and watch how their behavior changes. If you read something interesting, try it. If something doesn't work the way you expect, try variations until you can get what you want. Experimenting will make the commands stick in your memory so that next time you will have an idea how to use them.

## A.3   Finding Others Who Have Done It

If you have source code for your system (something which is unfortunately uncommon), look at how a tool which successfully does what you want to do accomplishes it. For example, figuring out how to do job control (a feature specific to Berkeley UNIX) can be difficult. Looking at the source for *csh* may provide hints about how to implement it.

Several shell scripts come with the system (finding them is discussed in Section 9.7). Look at them and see how they work.

USENET news (discussed in Section A.6) has several newsgroups which have source code freely available. Looking at the source code for the utilities which come across can often be a learning experience (although not everything that comes across is an example of how to do a good job of writing UNIX tools).

The Free Software Foundation is also a good place to obtain source code to many utilities. Their address is given in Chapter 1. The documentation for the code varies in quality, but some of it is better than the standard UNIX documentation.

## A.4   Other Books Which May Be Useful

No one book can cover everything; several books have been produced which do an excellent job of covering related topics that of this book. Unfortunately, there are also many poorly written books on UNIX available. The books listed here are well written and useful; some of these books have been mentioned other places in the text.

*Software Tools*[1] and its fraternal twin *Software Tools in Pascal*[2] by Brian Kernighan and P. J. Plauger present excellent discussions of why programs should be written as tools and how to write them.

*Programming Pearls*[3] by Jon Bentley uses short, interesting examples to teach good programming techniques and design principles. Based on essays that appeared in *Communications of the ACM*, this book should be required reading for all people who use computers for any sort of programming. Fast and fun reading, this book has lots of problems to help the reader develop insight while enjoying it. This book has a sequel, *More Programming Pearls: Confessions of a Coder.*[4]

Also by Jon Bentley is *Writing Efficient Programs.*[5] This book is a classic, and anyone interested in efficiency (everybody should be) should read this book. It is full of examples and real-life tales of problems and how they have been solved. Many problems help reinforce the concepts presented.

Changing the subject to more specifically UNIX, *The Design of the UNIX Operating System*[6] by Maurice Bach discusses in great detail how the kernel works and what happens when the system calls are used. The information in this book can lead to useful insight when programming with UNIX.

One layer out from Bach is *Advanced UNIX Programming*[7] by Marc Rochkind. Rochkind discusses the system calls and how to use them. This book is Section 2 of Volume 1 of the *UNIX Programmer's Manual* with the addition of many examples and explanation of what is going on.

A good book as an introduction to UNIX is *The UNIX Programming Environment* by Brian Kernighan and Rob Pike. This book covers many of the tools UNIX offers, stressing the use of tools to solve problems.

1. Addison-Wesley, 1976.
2. Addison-Wesley, 1981.
3. Addison-Wesley, 1986.
4. Addison-Wesley, 1988.
5. Prentice-Hall, 1982.
6. Prentice-Hall, 1986.
7. Prentice-Hall, 1985.

A definitive reference on the *awk* programming Language is *The AWK Programming Language*[8] by Alfred Aho, Brian Kernighan, and Peter Weinberger. Loaded with examples, this book shows how to use all of the features of the latest version of the language.

Finally, perhaps the best reference on the C programming language is *The C Programming Language*[9] by Brian Kernighan and Dennis Ritchie (referred to as K&R throughout the UNIX community). This book is the one which taught many people (including the author) the C programming language.

## A.5 Usenix and UniForum

Every year Usenix puts on two general and several more specialized conferences and UniForum[10] puts on one. These conferences are an excellent way to learn what is happening in the field. Usenix tends to be oriented more toward the technical side of UNIX, whereas UniForum is closer to the end users.

Both groups have tutorials at their major conferences taught by people who know the subject well. These tutorials are an excellent way to learn from the best, although there is no opportunity to immediately put the knowledge to use, since a system is not provided on which the students can experiment.

## A.6 USENET News

USENET is a loose network of thousands of machines throughout the world. At one time, USENET was exclusively for UNIX systems; now, however, a few other operating systems are represented. Most of the systems run some version of UNIX, however. USENET is divided into over 250 newsgroups where everything from food to movies is discussed. Some newsgroups contain source for new UNIX utilities, others the latest game. Of special note are the newsgroups

comp.unix   For general discussions about UNIX in general.

comp.unix.wizards   For discussions about the insides of UNIX, how something new should be accomplished, and bug reports for the system.

8. Addison-Wesley, 1988.
9. Prentice-Hall, 1978.
10. Formerly known as /usr/group.

comp.unix.questions   For asking and receiving many answers to UNIX questions.

comp.sources.unix   For source code for UNIX utilities. A small sample of the programs which have been posted here includes *watcher*, a public domain version of *tar*, shells, and a complex arithmetic library.

comp.sources.misc   For miscellaneous source code. Some of the programs posted here include a program to generate an ASCII chart in hex, decimal, and octal; a program to improve overstriking efficiency in *nroff* output; and a **malloc** package with debugging.

The UNIX discussion groups are excellent places to learn by listening. The source groups have no discussion but instead have source written by people in the UNIX community which is made available to all, free of charge. For example, *watcher* was made available through the newsgroup comp.sources.unix.

As mentioned earlier, USENET is a loose network. It has no central administration. The software was written by volunteers and placed in the public domain. Many of the connections between machines are over dial-up phone lines. All of this leads to a low-cost way of having conversations with people throughout the world. To join USENET you need to find a site which is willing to pass the news on to you. From them you get a copy of the software and install it on your machine (which can be quite a task, but it is beyond the scope of this book). Once you are connected, a good introduction to the net exists in the newsgroup news.announce.newusers, explaining etiquette and answering many of the questions frequently asked by newcomers to the net.

One way of joining USENET is to contact UUNET Communications. They can be reached at the following address.

UUNET Communications Services
3110 Fairview Park Drive, Suite 570
Falls Church, VA 22042
(703) 876-5050
uunet@uunet.uu.net

# Unformatted Manual Page for *watcher*

```
.de EX
.nf
.sp
.in +0.5i
..
.de NX
.sp
.in -0.5i
.ad
.fi
..
.TH WATCHER 1 "University of New Mexico CIRT"
\".UC 6
.ad
.SH NAME
watcher - system monitoring program
.SH SYNOPSIS
.BR watcher " [ " -p " ] [ " -v " ]"
.RB "[ " -h " histfile ] [ " -f " controlfile ]"
.SH DESCRIPTION
.I Watcher
is a program to watch the system, reporting only when it finds something
amiss.
.I Watcher
reads commands from
.I controlfile
to determine what to watch, the output format of the commands it is to
run, and the acceptable limits for the output of those commands.
If no
.B -f
option is present, the program looks first for 'watcherfile',
then 'Watcherfile' to use as the control file.
.PP
The
.B -h
.I histfile
```

flag tells watcher what file to use as a history file for comparisons
between runs. The default is 'watcher.history'.
.PP
The
.B -p
option has
.I watcher
pretty print the control file. This is useful to make sure that watcher
is parsing the file the way expected, and to provide a prettier version
of the control file to use (i.e., it is of limited use except when
debugging the parser).
.PP
The
.B -v
option tells watcher to be verbose as it is running. It will print out
various information about where it is looking for the files that it
uses, the commands that it is executing, and the output from these
commands. This option is mainly of use when debugging control files or
debugging watcher itself.
.PP
.I Watcherfile
contains a sequence of entries that specify the commands to be executed,
the output format of those commands, and what changes should be
reported. The format of the control file is one or more of the
following:
.EX
( <pipeline> ) { <alias> }
        <output format> :
        <change format>.
.NX
A <pipeline> is a series of commands joined together with pipes ('pipe').
This command is executed and the output parsed according to the output
format specified. It is then checked against the change format for
potential problems. An <alias> is optional; it is used when identifying
the command in the report of problems encountered. If there is no
alias, the entire pipeline is used. The reason for using an alias is
to keep the report clean; the pipelines tend to be long and messy.
.PP
An <output format> is either a column format or a relative format. A
column format is one or more of the following:
.EX
        <start> - <end> <name> % <type>
.NX
Where <start> is the first column containing the information to be compared and
<end> is the last one. <name> is the name of the field. This name is
matched with the names in the change format to identify where in the
output the appropriate information is. <type> is either "d", "f", "s", or
"k" specifying integer, floating point, or string data, or a keyword
which is used in matching output from the various programs between runs.
.PP

Relative formats are one or more of the following:
.EX
<field> <name> % <type>
.NX
Where <field> is the field on the line (a field is defined as a sequence
of non-whitespace surrounded by whitespace). <name> and <type> are the
same as for above.
.PP
A change format consists of various names and what changes are
allowable. Change format entries are separated by semicolons (';'). The
list of change formats is terminated by a period ('.'). A semicolon
does not follow the last change format.
.I Watcher
knows about five types of changes. It can compare the output (numeric)
to the previous value and calculate the percentage change. If the
change is greater than a set amount, a message is generated. The syntax
of this format is:
.EX
        <name> <value> %
.NX
where <name> is a name matching a name in the output format and <value>
is the maximum percentage change which is allowed before a report is
issued.
.PP
Very similar to the percentage change is the absolute change. The only
difference is that a percentage is not calculated. The difference is
calculated and compared to the value given. Values greater than what is
provided are reported. The syntax is:
.EX
        <name> <value>
.NX
.PP
A maximum and minimum may be specified for numeric data also. This is
useful for only numeric data. The format for this is:
.EX
        <name> <max> <min>
.NX
.PP
.I Watcher
can also watch for string values changing from a given value to any
other value. This syntax is:
.EX
        <name>"<value>"
.NX
or
.EX
        <name>"<value>","<value2>"
.NX
where the second case checks the string value against all of the values
provided and only if it matches none is a message produced.
.PP

The last change
.I watcher
can watch for is any change at all. The syntax is:
.EX
   &lt;name&gt;
.NX
.PP
A sample control file is provided below:
.EX
(df -i pipe /usr/ucb/tail +2) { df }
    1-9 filesystem%k 41-42 spaceused%d 64-65 inodesused%d 1-9 device%k:
      spaceused 15%;
      spaceused 0 89;
      inodesused 15%;
      inodesused 0 49.
(/usr/ucb/ruptime pipe fgrep -f UnmHosts) { ruptime }
    2 status%s 1 machine%k 7 loadav%d:
      loadav 0 10;
      status "up".
(ps -aux pipe fgrep -v -f Daemons pipe /usr/ucb/tail +2) { 'ps with no daemons' }
    9-14 pid%k 16-19 percentcpu%d 42-45 cputime%d:
      cputime 0 10.
.NX
Note that there is no order for the output format specifiers; the second
field may be specified before the first.
.PP
All names are of arbitrary length, start with [a-zA-Z] and contain no
white space unless enclosed in tics ( " ' " ).
.PP
The pipeline is executed by
.I popen(3),
which uses
.I sh(1)
to expand the command; therefore shell metacharacters may be used.
.PP
The control file may have comments in it. Comments are delimited by a \#
on the left and a newline on the right.
.SH FILES
.nf
Watcherfile or watcherfile       default control file.
watcher.history      default file containing results of previous run.

.SH AUTHOR
.nf
Kenneth Ingham
Computing and Information Resources and Technology
University of New Mexico
2701 Campus NE
Albuquerque, NM, 87131
ingham@unm.edu
.SH "SEE ALSO"

popen(3), sh(1),
.I Keeping Watch over the
.I Flocks by Night (and day)
by Kenneth Ingham, Summer 1987 Usenix proceedings.
.SH DIAGNOSTICS
Files which can't be opened cause a message about which files couldn't
be found and the program exits.
.sp
There are various syntax errors when parsing the controlfile. These
also cause an exit.
.sp
.I Watcher
complains when output does not parse according to the format
provided. It will continue to look at the rest of the output.
.SH BUGS
Doesn't warn when a string variable has been selected for a numeric
comparison.

# Formatted Manual Page for *watcher*

Due to differences between typesetting a book and a manual page, the manual page presented here will not be identical to what would be printed if the manual page were typeset separately. The major difference is in the page headers and footers.

WATCHER(1)          UNIX Programmer's Manual          WATCHER(1)

**NAME**
  watcher - system monitoring program

**SYNOPSIS**
  **watcher** [ **-p** ] [ **-v** ] [ **-h** histfile ] [ **-f** controlfile ]

**DESCRIPTION**
  *Watcher* is a program to watch the system, reporting only when it finds something amiss. *Watcher* reads commands from *controlfile* to determine what to watch, the output format of the commands it is to run, and the acceptable limits for the output of those commands. If no **-f** option is present, the program looks first for 'watcherfile', then 'Watcherfile' to use as the control file.

  The **-h** *histfile* flag tells watcher what file to use as a history file for comparisons between runs. The default is 'watcher.history'.

  The **-p** option has *watcher* pretty print the control file. This is useful to make sure that watcher is parsing the file the way expected, and to provide a prettier version of the control file to use (i.e., it is of limited use except when debugging the parser).

  The **-v** option tells watcher to be verbose as it is running. It will print out various information about where it is looking for the files that it uses, the commands that it is executing, and the output from these commands. This option is mainly of use when debugging control files or debugging watcher itself.

*Watcherfile* contains a sequence of entries that specify the commands to be executed, the output format of those commands, and what changes should be reported. The format of the control file is one or more of the following:

```
( <pipeline> ) { <alias> }
      <output format> :
      <change format>.
```

A <pipeline> is a series of commands joined together with pipes (|). This command is executed and the output parsed according to the output format specified. It is then checked against the change format for potential problems. An <alias> is optional; it is used when identifying the command in the report of problems encountered. If there is no alias, the entire pipeline is used. The reason for using an alias is to keep the report clean; the pipelines tend to be long and messy.

An <output format> is either a column format or a relative format. A column format is one or more of the following:

```
<start> - <end> <name> % <type>
```

Where <start> is the first column containing the information to be compared and <end> is the last one. <name> is the name of the field. This name is matched with the names in the change format to identify where in the output the appropriate information is. <type> is either "d", "f", "s", or "k" specifying integer, floating point, or string data, or a keyword which is used in matching output from the various programs between runs.

Relative formats are one or more of the following:

```
<field> <name> % <type>
```

Where <field> is the field on the line (a field is defined as a sequence of non-whitespace surrounded by whitespace). <name> and <type> are the same as for above.

A change format consists of various names and what changes are allowable. Change format entries are separated by semicolons (';'). The list of change formats is terminated by a period ('.'). A semicolon does not follow the last change format. *Watcher* knows about five types of changes. It can compare the output (numeric) to the previous value and calculate the percentage change. If the change is greater than a set amount, a message is generated. The syntax of this format is

```
<name> <value> %
```

where <name> is a name matching a name in the output format and
<value> is the maximum percentage change which is allowed before
a report is issued.

Very similar to the percentage change is the absolute change. The
only difference is that a percentage is not calculated. The difference is
calculated and compared to the value given. Values greater than what
is provided are reported. The syntax is

```
<name> <value>
```

A maximum and minimum may be specified for numeric data
also. This is useful for only numeric data. The format for this is

```
<name> <max> <min>
```

*Watcher* can also watch for string values changing from a given
value to any other value. This syntax is

```
<name> "<value>"
```

or

```
<name> "<value>" , "<value2>"
```

where the second case checks the string value against all of the values
provided and only if it matches none is a message produced.

The last change *watcher* can watch for is any change at all. The
syntax is

```
<name>
```

A sample control file is provided below:

```
(df -i | /usr/ucb/tail +2) { df }
        1-9 filesystem%k 41-42 spaceused%d 64-65 inodesused%d 1-9 device%k;
                spaceused 15%;
                spaceused 0 89;
                inodesused 15%,
                inodesused 0 49.
(/usr/ucb/ruptime | fgrep -f UnmHosts) { ruptime }
        2 status%s 1 machine%k 7 loadav%d:
                loadav 0 10;
                status "up".
(ps -aux | fgrep -v -f Daemons | /usr/ucb/tail +2) { 'ps with no daemons' }
        9-14 pid%k 16-19 percentcpu%d 42-45 cputime%d:
                cputime 0 10.
```

Note that there is no order for the output format specifiers; the second field may be specified before the first.

All names are of arbitrary length, start with [a-zA-Z] and contain no white space unless enclosed in tics ( " ' " ).

The pipeline is executed by *popen(3)*, which uses *sh(1)* to expand the command; therefore shell metacharacters may be used.

The control file may have comments in it. Comments are delimited by a # on the left and a newline on the right.

## FILES

| | |
|---|---|
| Watcherfile or watcherfile | default control file. |
| watcher.history | default file containing results of previous run. |

## AUTHOR

Kenneth Ingham
Computing and Information Resources and Technology
University of New Mexico
2701 Campus NE
Albuquerque, NM, 87131
ingham@unm.edu

## SEE ALSO

popen(3), sh(1), *Keeping Watch over the Flocks by Night (and day)* by Kenneth Ingham, Summer 1987 Usenix proceedings.

## DIAGNOSTICS

Files which can't be opened cause a message about which files couldn't be found and the program exits.

There are various syntax errors when parsing the controlfile. These also cause an exit.

*Watcher* complains when output does not parse according to the format provided. It will continue to look at the rest of the output.

## BUGS

Doesn't warn when a string variable has been selected for a numeric comparison.

# Paper on *watcher* **Presented at Usenix**

### Keeping watch over the flocks
### by night (and day)

Kenneth Ingham
University of New Mexico Computing Center
Distributed Systems Group
2701 Campus NE
Albuquerque, NM 87131
(505) 277-8044
ingham@ariel.unm.edu or ucbvax!unmvax!ariel!ingham

### Abstract

Over the last several years, the number of machines maintained by the University of New Mexico Computing Center has increased rapidly, yet the number of system managers monitoring these systems has remained static. Consequently, the system managers were faced with the task of watching more and more machines; since only one system manager is on call at any time (known affectionately as "DOC"), this soon proved to be an unacceptable situation. Shell scripts running every six hours gave some assistance; this was offset by the fact that the scripts generated a great deal of output indicating normal system operation, which the system manager still had to scan carefully for signs of trouble. This paper describes *watcher*, a flexible system monitor which watches the system more closely than the human system manager while generating less output for him to examine.

Running more often than the above mentioned set of shell scripts, *watcher* is able to keep closer tabs on the system; since it delivers only a list of potential problems, however, this extra monitoring produces no corresponding increase in the demand on DOC. No problems slip by unnoticed in the more concise output, leading to an improvement in overall system availability as well as the more effective utilization of the system manager's time.

## 0. Acknowledgments (I couldn't have done it without you)

I would like to thank Leslie Gorsline for her assistance in the writing of this paper. Without her, this paper might not have been. Also thanks to the UNMCC distributed systems group for their comments that helped improve *watcher*.

## 1. Background (the problem)

The computing facilities offered by the University of New Mexico Computing Center (UNMCC) include three microvaxen, five large vaxen (780 or bigger), and a Sequent B8000. In addition to these Unix/VMS machines, the UNMCC Distributed Systems Group (DSG) monitors a number of the various microvaxen and sun workstations scattered across campus. This duty falls to the DSG Programmer designated as "DOC", or "DSG On Call", who receives his beeper based on a monthly rotation schedule.

In the past, shell scripts running every six hours reported various system statistics to DOC, who then scanned the output for signs of possible trouble. The output of these shell scripts became overwhelming as the number of machines and potential problems grew; corresponding to this increase in output was an increase in the amount of time that DOC had to spend reading this output. In addition, most of this output merely indicated normal system operation; potential problems were buried amongst non-problems. Because of this, DOC could often waste a tremendous amount of time wading through system status reports, time which can be better spent actually fixing system problems.

Unix is equipped with many powerful tools for program development, but none which simply watch the system for signs of trouble. Programs like *ps* and *df* provide information regarding the current state of the machine, yet it still remains DOC's responsibility to interpret this information and assess the health of the system at any given time. This deficiency can be rectified by providing the system with the capacity to determine its own state of health, advising DOC when it notices a problem which requires DOC's intervention.

## 2. Design Goals (devising the solution)

In designing *watcher*, the author closely examined just what DOC does in monitoring the system; just how does DOC spot potential trouble in the DOC reports? These reports consist of output from *df -i*, *ruptime, ps -aux | sort*, and the tail of *cronlog*, which usually only changes in the middle of the night. It was determined that DOC's task consisted primarily of scanning various numbers in this output, deciding whether or not they had exceeded an allowable maximum or minimum, or if the values had changed too much from the last time the command was run, assuming the last value is even remembered. Getting a computer to do this is more complicated than might seem at first glance, due to inconsistencies in the location of pertinent information between runs of these commands. For instance, the process occupying the fifth line of *ps -ax* might next time appear on the eighth line; similarly, *uptime* does not consistently put germane information in the same place on the line.

While flexibility is certainly a primary design consideration, it is not the whole story. In order to improve DOC's effectiveness, the program should run frequently, roughly every two or three hours, catching problems early (hopefully before they have affected the users). Thus, the program should also be as silent as possible except when it detects a potential problem; any advantage DOC gains in using *watcher* would be eliminated if the program delivered an exceedingly verbose status report every two hours. *watcher*'s problem reports should be exact and concise, leading DOC immediately to the trouble.

The problem of reducing the amount of output DOC must process can be approached in different ways, including the redesign of the current shell scripts. A simple *awk* script can watch the output from *df* [1]. However, each command would require a custom tailored *awk* script to look at it. This task grows more complicated as the number of programs running increases. While a program could be written to generate these *awk* scripts, this process is needlessly complex; for only a bit more work, an efficient C program such as *watcher* can be developed.

## 3. Design (actual implementation of the solution)

Run at intervals specified in *crontab*, *watcher* parses a control file (*./watcherfile* by default) with a *yacc* generated parser, building a data structure containing all of the information from the file. The file contains the list of commands *watcher* should run (the pipeline), output specifications for each command (the output format), and the guidelines used in determining if something is amiss and should be reported to DOC (the change format). A sample *watcher* control file would look something like this (comment lines begin with a '#'):

```
# Here is the pipeline and its alias:
(df -i | /usr/ucb/tail +2) { df }
# the output format; this is a column output format:
        $1-9 device%k $41-42 spaceused%d $64-65 inodesused%d:
# and the change format:
                spaceused 15%;
                spaceused 0 89;
                inodesused 15%;
                inodesused 0 49.


# another command example:
(/usr/ucb/ruptime | fgrep -f UnmHosts) { ruptime }
# this is a relative output format
        2 status%s 1 machine%k 7 loadav%d:
# and another change format:
                loadav 0 10;
                status "up".
```

The first entry causes *watcher* to run the *df* pipeline listed in parentheses. When reporting problems, *watcher* refers to this command by the alias provided in the braces; if no alias appears, *watcher* uses the entire pipeline.

The output format instructs *watcher* how to parse the output; column format, indicated in the output format by **num-num,** instructs *watcher* that the output should be parsed by columns, while relative format, denoted by a single integer, shows that the output should be broken up by whitespaces. Through the convention **name%type,** the output format also names each field, indicating whether the field is numeric, string, or keyword, specified by **d, s,** or **k** respectively. Keyword fields are used to match up corresponding output lines between runs. Thus

```
41-42 spaceused%d
```

indicates that this field, named **spaceused,** contains numeric information in columns 41−42, while

```
2 status%s
```

informs *watcher* that the second word (group of non-whitespace characters) on the line is a string field named **status.** For the *df* example
given above,

```
Filesystem kbytes   used avail  capacity  iused ifree %iused Mounted on
/dev/hp1f    52431 39763  7424     84%      6937  9447  42%    /develop
```

**device** would be */dev/hp1f,* **spaceused** would be 84, and **inodesused**
would be 42. Similarly, the output from the *ruptime* example, which
looks like this

```
charon            up 26+07:53,       17 users,       load 3.12, 2.90, 2.66
```

would be broken at the following places:

```
charon | up | 26+07:53, | 17 | users, | load | 3.12, | 2.90, | 2.66,
```

assigning up to **status,** and 3.12 to **loadav.**

The name field also appears in the change format, designating allowable values for this field to have. These values can be specified as
single character strings in the case of string fields; in the case of numeric fields, the values take the form of either percentage or absolute
changes, or a minimum and maximum which delineate an acceptable
range. Thus

```
inodesused 15%;
inodesused 0 49.
```

signifies that DOC should be notified if the field named **inodesused**
increases by more than 15% from the last run, or if it is outside the
range 0 to 49; similarly

```
status "up";
```

informs *watcher* to notify DOC if the **status** field contains anything
other than the word up.

As *watcher* parses the output of a pipeline, it stores the pertinent
parts of the output in a history file (by default, *./watcher.history*). The
next time *watcher* runs, it reads this file to provide comparison values
for the command. If a command is new (i.e. it has no previously-
stored output in the history file), *watcher* checks the fields which require no previous data, such as min-max fields, while still storing *all*
of the relevant information to the history file. Thus, the next time the

new command is run, it will be an *old* command, and meaningful between-run comparisons can be made.

When *watcher* detects no problems with the system, DOC receives an empty mail message with the subject "*hostname* had no problems at *date*"; this is to insure that *mail* is running correctly. When it notices a problem which should be brought to DOC's attention, it mails the system problem report in a concise format, explaining what is wrong and why. Thus, rather than the megabytes of shell script output that DOC used to receive and have to read, he merely sees this when he reads his mail:

```
Mail version 5.2 6/21/85. Type ? for help.
"/usr/spool/mail/ingham": 5 messages 5 new
 N 1 root@charon.unm Sat Apr 11 16:00 8/212 "charon had no problems
     at Sat Apr 11 16:00"
 N 2 root@ariel.unm Sat Apr 11 16:00 8/208 "ariel had no problems at
     Sat Apr 11 16:00"
 N 3 root@geinah.unm Sat Apr 11 16:00 11/417 "System problem report
     for geinah at Sat Apr 11 16:00"
 N 4 root@izar.unm Sat Apr 11 16:00 8/204 "izar had no problems at Sat
     Apr 11 16:00"
 N 5 root@deimos.unm Sat Apr 11 16:00 8/212 "deimos had no problems at
     Sat Apr 11 16:00"
```

The letters indicating no problems can be immediately deleted, and DOC can turn his attention to the letter indicating a system problem. A sample problem report would look something like this:

```
df has a max/min value out of range:
/dev/hp0h 140488 111195 15244 91% 10145 28767 26% /us
where spaceused = 91.00; valid range 0.00 to 89.00.
Also it had inodesused change by more than 10%.
Previous value 20.00; current value 26.00.
```

Note that if a line has more than one indication of a problem, all anomalies are included in the report. This provides DOC with as much information as possible, allowing him to determine the problem quickly and devise a rapid fix (hopefully before users know something is amiss).

## 4. Results (how it has helped us)

*watcher*'s primary advantage lies in the reduction of DOC's work load. It has taken over the more menial aspects of monitoring a system, tasks like reading and comparing numbers, giving DOC more time to concentrate on bugs of a nature which *watcher* isn't set up to monitor, such as problems in the accounting system. DOC is apprised of potential problems quickly, and in some cases can repair them in less time than simply reading the shell script output would have taken.

The ability to monitor changes between runs has also helped bring to our attention some problems which were missed in the DOC reports. For example, disk space on /u2 on one of our machines jumped by more than 15%. However, this jump did not force the total space used above 90 inodes. If DOC would have investigated the filesystem, it is unlikely that DOC would have even noticed this sudden change. The facility to watch for relative changes between runs enables DOC to catch problems in their infancy, and fix problems such as filesystems filling up too rapidly before they inconvenience the users.

Since the system manager specifies not only the commands *watcher* will execute and the time lapse between successive runs, but also the parameters which indicate system anomalies, *watcher* can easily be seen as a very flexible, general system monitor. Its use at UNM has provided an increase in the productivity of the system manager, which has led in turn to the increase in the reliability and availability of the systems at UNMCC.

## 5.  Availability (how to get one)

*watcher* will be sent to the moderator of mod.sources after the conference is over.

## 6.  References (you might also find this interesting)

[1] Monitoring Free Disk Space, Rik Farrow, Wizard's Grabbag, *Unix World*, Vol. IV, no. 3, pp. 86–87.

# Code for *watcher*

/* Cyylex.c
yylex for watcher: this is a simple routine looking for numbers, special characters and strings. The special chars are stored in 'words' and represent tokens by themselves. In y.tab.h are the values to return for the various tokens which are not listed in 'words'.

Kenneth Ingham

Copyright (C) 1987 The University of New Mexico
*/

```c
#include "defs.h"
#include "y.tab.h"

char words[] = "\".,* | ;:%@$-{}";

yylex()
{
        int c, i;
        static char str[MAX_STR];
        int real;

        while (isspace(c = getchar()))
                ;

                if (c == EOF)
                        return EOF;

                if (c == '(') {/* aha, pipeline */
                        c = getchar();
                        for (i=0; c != EOF && c != ')'; i++) {
                                str[i] = c;
                                c = getchar();
                        }
                        str[i] = '\0';
                        if (c == EOF) {
                                fprintf(stderr, "Missing ')' to end pipeline.\n");
```

```
                        return EOF;
                }
                yylval.str = strsave(str);
                return PIPELINE;
        }

        if (c == '#') { /* comment to end of line */
                while (c != '\n' && c != EOF)
                        c = getchar();
                if (c == EOF)
                        return EOF;
                return yylex();
        }

        if (index(words, c) != 0)
                return c;

        if (c == '+' pipepipe c == '-' pipepipe isdigit(c)) { /* a number */

                real = False;
                i = 0;
                str[i++] = c;

do {
        str[i++] = getchar();
        if (str[i-1] == '.')
                real = True;
} while (isdigit(str[i-1]) pipepipe str[i-1] == '.');
(void) ungetchar(str[i-1]);
str[i-1] = '\0';
if (real) {
        yylval.real = (float) atof(str);
        return FLOAT;
}
else {
        yylval.integer = atoi(str);
        return INTEGER;
}
}

if (c == '\' ') { /* literal string */
        c = getchar();
        for (i=0; c != EOF && c != '\' '; i++) {
                str[i] = c;
                c = getchar();
        }
        str[i] = '\0';
        yylval.str = strsave(str);
        return STRING;
}
```

```
/* nothing else matched. Must be plain string (whitespace sep) */

for (i=1, str[0]=c; c != EOF && !isspace(c) && !index(words,c); i++) {

        c = getchar();
        str[i] = c;
}
(void) ungetchar(c);
str[i-1] = '\0';
                        yylval.str = strsave(str);
                        return STRING;

        }
```

```
/*
abs_check: verify that the value has not changed more than the
allowed absolute amount.

Kenneth Ingham

Copyright (C) 1988 The University of New Mexico
*/

#include "defs.h"
#include "y.tab.h"

abs_check(current, prev_val, allowable, cmd, name, line)
char *current;
double allowable;
struct everything *prev_val;
char *cmd, *name, *line;
{
        extern int line_ok;
        double change, previous, value;
        double to_double();

        previous = to_double(prev_val);
        value = atof(current);

        change = value - previous;
        if (change > allowable) {
            if (line_ok) {
                printf("%s had %s change by more than %.2f.\n",

                        cmd, name, allowable);
                printf("%s\n",line);
            }
            else {
                printf("Also, it had %s change by more than %.2f.\n",
```

```
                    name, allowable);
          }
          printf("Previous value %.2f; ",previous);
          printf("current value %.2f.\n", value);
          line_ok = False;
       }
}


/*
any_check: check a value and make sure it has not changed at all.

Kenneth Ingham

Copyright (C) 1988 The University of New Mexico
*/

#include "defs.h"

any_check(value, last, cmd, name, line)
char *value;
struct everything *last;
char *cmd, *name, *line;
{
          extern int line_ok;
          char *to_string(), *previous;

          previous = to_string(last);
          if (strcmp(value, previous) != 0) {
               if (line_ok) {
                    printf("%s has a value which changed:\n", cmd);

                    printf("%s\n",line);
               }
               else
                    printf("Also, it had a string value change:\n");

               printf("where %s = '%s'; it was '%s'", name, value, previous);

               printf("\n");
               line_ok = False;
          }
}


/*
baderr: A bad error has been caught. Print an error message explaining

          why we are dying, then exit.
```

Assumptions:

the signal number in sig is an actual signal number and has an

entry in sys_siglist (BSD ONLY).

Arguments:

sig: the number of the signal which brought us here.

Author:

Kenneth Ingham

Copyright (C) 1987 The University of New Mexico

```
*/

#include "defs.h"

baderr(sig)
int sig;
{
#ifdef BSD
        extern char *sys_siglist[];

        printf(">> Unrecoverable error. %s Bye. <<\n",sys_siglist[sig]);

#else
        printf(">> Unrecoverable error. Signal %d. Bye. <<\n", sig);

#endif
        exit(1);
}



/*
build_abs: build an absolute change format for the parser.

Kenneth Ingham

Copyright (C) 1988 The University of New Mexico
*/

#include "defs.h"
#include "y.tab.h"

struct change_fmt_st *
build_abs(string, number)
struct number *number;
char *string:
{
        struct change_fmt_st *p;
```

```
        p = allocate(struct change_fmt_st);
        p->name = string;
        p->fmt.fmt.abs_amount = number->type == INTEGER ?
                (double)number->value.integer : number->value.real;
        p->fmt.type = ABSOLUTE;

        return p;
}



/*
build_any: build an any change structure for the parser.

Kenneth Ingham

Copyright (C) 1988 The University of New Mexico
*/

#include "defs.h"
#include "y.tab.h"

struct change_fmt_st *
build_any(string)
char *string;
{
        struct change_fmt_st *p;

        p = allocate(struct change_fmt_st);
        p->name = string;
        p->fmt.type = ANY;

        return p;
}



/*
build_cmd: build one command structure from the pieces provided.

Kenneth Ingham

Copyright (C) 1988 The University of New Mexico
*/

#include "defs.h"
#include "y.tab.h"

struct cmd_st *
build_cmd(pipeline, alias, out_fmt, change_fmt)
char *alias, *pipeline;
```

```
struct out_fmt_st *out_fmt;
struct change_fmt_st *change_fmt;
{
        extern struct out_fmt_st *key;
        struct cmd_st *p;

        p = allocate(struct cmd_st);

        p->pipeline = pipeline;
        p->alias = alias;
        p->change_fmt = change_fmt;
        p->next = NULL;
        p->out_fmt = out_fmt;
        p->key = key;
        key = NULL;

        return p;
}


/*
build_col: build a column out structure for the parser.

Kenneth Ingham

Copyright (C) 1988 The University of New Mexico
*/

#include "defs.h"
#include "y.tab.h"

struct col_out_st *
build_col(start, end, name, type)
char *name, *type;
int start, end;
{
        extern struct out_fmt_st *key;
        extern int parse_error;
        extern char *myname;
        struct col_out_st *p;

        p = allocate(struct col_out_st);
        p->name = name;
        p->start = start;
        p->end = end;
        p->next = NULL;

        if (type[1] != '\0' pipepipe index("dfsk", type[0]) == NULL) {

                fprintf(stderr,"%s: Invalid type specifier ", myname);
```

```
        fprintf(stderr,"'%s' for '%s' (col fmt).\n", type, p->name);

        fprintf(stderr,"Expecting one of 'dfsk'\n");
        parse_error = True;
        return p;
    }

    switch (*type) {
        case 'd':
            p->type = INTEGER;
            break;
        case 'f':
            p->type = FLOAT;
            break;
        case 's':
            p->type = STRING;
            break;
        case 'k':
            p->type = KEY;
            key = allocate(struct out_fmt_st);
            key->out_fmt.col_fmt = p;
            key->type = COLUMN;
            break;
        default:
            /* checked above in if */
            fprintf(stderr,"Impossible condition in build_col\n");

            exit(1);
    }

    if (start > end) {
        fprintf(stderr,"%s: start %d larger than end %d!\n",

            myname, start, end);
        parse_error = True;
    }

    return p;
}


/*
build_maxmin: build a max/min format for the parser.

Kenneth Ingham

Copyright (C) 1988 The University of New Mexico
*/

#include "defs.h"
#include "y.tab.h"
```

```
struct change_fmt_st *
build_maxmin(string, min, max)
struct number *max, *min;
char *string;
{
        struct change_fmt_st *p;

        p = allocate(struct change_fmt_st);
        p->name = string;
        p->fmt.fmt.max_min.max = max->type == INTEGER ?
                (double)max->value.integer : max->value.real;
        p->fmt.fmt.max_min.min = min->type == INTEGER ?
                (double)min->value.integer : min->value.real;
        p->fmt.type = MAX_MIN;

        return p;
}



/*
build_pct: build a percent change format for the parser.

Kenneth Ingham

Copyright (C) 1988 The University of New Mexico
*/

#include "defs.h"
#include "y.tab.h"

struct change_fmt_st *
build_pct(string, number)
struct number *number;
char *string;
{
        struct change_fmt_st *p;

        p = allocate(struct change_fmt_st);
        p->fmt.type = PERCENT;
        p->name = string;
        if (number->type == INTEGER)
                p->fmt.fmt.percent = (float)number->value.integer / 100.0;

        else
                p->fmt.fmt.percent = number->value.real / 100.0;

        free((char *)number);

        return p;
}
```

```c
/*
build_rel: build a relative output format structure for the parser

Kenneth Ingham

Copyright (C) 1988 The University of New Mexico
*/

#include "defs.h"
#include "y.tab.h"

struct rel_out_st *
build_rel(field, name, type)
char *name, *type;
int field;
{
        extern struct out_fmt_st *key;
        extern int parse_error;
        extern char *myname;
        struct rel_out_st *p;

        p = allocate(struct rel_out_st);
        p->name = name;
        p->field = field;
        p->next = NULL;

        if (type[1] != '\0' pipepipe index("dfsk", type[0]) == NULL) {

                fprintf(stderr,"%s: Invalid type specifier ", myname);

                fprintf(stderr,"'%s' for '%s' (rel fmt).\n", type, p->name);

                fprintf(stderr, "Expecting one of 'dfsk'\n");
                parse_error = True;
                return p;
        }

        switch (type[0]) {
            case 'd':
                p->type = INTEGER;
                break;
            case 'f':
                p->type = FLOAT;
                break;
            case 's':
                p->type = STRING;
                break;
            case 'k':
                p->type = KEY;
                key = allocate(struct out_fmt_st);
```

```
                    key->out_fmt.rel_fmt = p;
                    key->type = COLUMN;
                    break;
                default:
                    /* checked in if above */
                    fprintf(stderr,"impossible condition in build_rel\n");

                    exit(1);
        }

        return p;
}



/*
build_str: build a string format structure for the parser.

Kenneth Ingham

Copyright (C) 1988 The University of New Mexico
*/

#include "defs.h"
#include "y.tab.h"

struct change_fmt_st *
build_str(string, sarray)
char **sarray;
char *string;
{
        struct change_fmt_st *p;

        p = allocate(struct change_fmt_st);
        p->name = string;
        p->fmt.type = STRING;
        p->fmt.fmt.str_value = sarray;

        return p;
}



/*
check_col_item: find the part of the line corresponding to check.
Also find the previous results corresponding to the key for this line
(if any). Pass all of this to check_item.

Kenneth Ingham

Copyright (C) 1988 The University of New Mexico
*/
```

```
#include "defs.h"

check_col_item(prev_res, col_fmt, key_val, line, cf, cmd_name, hf)
struct old_cmd_st *prev_res;
struct col_out_st *col_fmt;
char *key_val, *line;
struct change_fmt_st *cf;
char *cmd_name;
FILE *hf;
{
        struct everything *prev_value;
        char tchar();
        char value[MAX_STR];

        find_prev_value(prev_res, col_fmt->name, key_val, &prev_value);

        if (get_col_field(line, col_fmt->start, col_fmt->end, value) != NULL)

            check_item(cf, value, cmd_name, line, prev_value);

        /*
        save the value in the history file for future comparisons.
        */
        if (*key_val)
            fprintf(hf, "\t\t%s %c %s\n", cf->name, tchar(col_fmt->type),

                value);
}


/*
check_item: given a value and a change format structure, make sure
that the value is in range.

Basically, this routine is a large switch statement on the type of
change that grabs the necessary info, and checks to see if the item
is worth mentioning.

Note that what we print out depends on whether or not something else

has been found wrong on this line.

Kenneth Ingham

Copyright (C) 1987 The University of New Mexico
*/

#include "defs.h"
#include "y.tab.h"
```

```
check_item(cf, value, cmd, line, prev_val)
char *value, *cmd, *line;
struct change_fmt_st *cf;
struct everything *prev_val;
{
        extern int line_ok, cmd_ok;

        switch(cf->fmt.type) {
            case PERCENT:
                if (prev_val == NULL) /* nothing to compare with */

                        return;
                pct_check(value, prev_val, cf->fmt.fmt.percent,
                    cmd, cf->name, line);
                break;
            case ABSOLUTE:
                if (prev_val == NULL) /* nothing to compare with */

                        return;
                abs_check(value, prev_val, cf->fmt.fmt.abs_amount,
                    cmd, cf->name, line);
                break;
            case MAX_MIN:
                maxmin_check(value, cf->fmt.fmt.max_min.max,
                    cf->fmt.fmt.max_min.min, cmd, cf->name, line);

                break;
            case STRING:
                str_check(value, cf->fmt.fmt.str_value, cmd,
                    cf->name, line);
                break;
            case ANY:
                if (prev_val == NULL) /* nothing to compare with */

                        return;
                any_check(value, prev_val, cmd, cf->name, line);
                break;
            default:
                printf("check_item: impossible condition\n");
                break;
        }
        cmd_ok = line_ok;
}


/*
check_rel_item: find the part of the line corresponding to check.
Also find the previous results corresponding to the key for this line
(if any). Pass all of this to check_item
```

Kenneth Ingham

```
#include "defs.h"

check_rel_item(prev_res, rel_fmt, key_val, line, cf, cmd_name, hf)
struct old_cmd_st *prev_res;
struct rel_out_st *rel_fmt;
char *key_val, *line;
struct change_fmt_st *cf;
char *cmd_name;
FILE *hf;
{
        struct everything *prev_value;
        char tchar();
        char value[MAX_STR];

        find_prev_value(prev_res, rel_fmt->name, key_val, &prev_value);

        if (get_rel_field(line, rel_fmt->field, value) != NULL)
            check_item(cf, value, cmd_name, line, prev_value);

        /*
        save the value in the history file for future comparisons.
        */
        if (*key_val)
            fprintf(hf, "\t\t%s %c %s\n", cf->name, tchar(rel_fmt->type),

                value);
}
```

```
/*
checkline: check the input line just read in against what we expect
to find and report any problems. Actually, most of the work is done
by check_item. We just identify what needs to be checked.
```

Kenneth Ingham

```
#include "defs.h"
#include "y.tab.h"

checkline(cmd, line, prev_res, hf)
struct cmd_st *cmd;
char *line;
struct old_cmd_st *prev_res;
```

```
FILE *hf;
{
        extern int line_ok;
        struct change_fmt_st *cf;
        struct out_fmt_st of;
        char key_val[MAX_STR];
        char *cmd_name;

        cmd_name = ((cmd->alias != NULL) ? cmd->alias : cmd->pipeline);

        save_key(cmd, line, key_val, hf); /* side effect: return key value */

        /* for each change format item */
        line_ok = True;
        for (cf=cmd->change_fmt; cf; cf=cf->next) {
            /* find the output format entry for this item */
            if (!find_of(cf->name, cmd->out_fmt, &of)) {
                fprintf(stderr, "Warning: %s appears in change list ",
                    cf->name);
                fprintf(stderr, "but not in output format for %s\n",

                    cmd_name);
                continue;
            }

            /*
            check the item, depending on which type of output
            format we have.
            */
            switch (cmd->out_fmt->type) {
                case RELATIVE:
                    check_rel_item(prev_res, of.out_fmt.rel_fmt,
                        key_val, line, cf, cmd_name, hf);
                    break;
                case COLUMN:
                    check_col_item(prev_res, of.out_fmt.col_fmt,
                        key_val, line, cf, cmd_name, hf);
                    break;
            }
        }
        if (!line_ok)
            printf("---------\n");
}


/*
the grammar describing the control file for watcher.

Kenneth Ingham

Copyright (C) 1987 The University of New Mexico
*/
```

```
%token PIPELINE FLOAT INTEGER STRING QUOTED_STRING

%start command

%{
#include "defs.h"
extern struct cmd_st *clist;
extern int control_line, parse_error;
int nslist = 0;
struct cmd_st *build_cmd();
struct rel_out_st *build_rel();
struct col_out_st *build_col();
struct change_fmt_st *build_pct(), *build_abs();
struct change_fmt_st *build_maxmin(), *build_str();
struct change_fmt_st *build_any();

#define add_end(type, start, what, assignto)     {\
                          type *p; \
                          for (p=(start); p->next != NULL; p = p->next)\
                               ;\
                          p->next = (what);\
                          assignto = start; }
%}

%union {
        struct cmd_st *cmd;
        struct col_out_st *cos;
        struct rel_out_st *ros;
        struct change_fmt_st *cfs;
        struct out_fmt_st *of;
        char **strarray;
        char *str;
        char chr;
        int integer;
        struct number *np;
        float real;
}

%type <str>          PIPELINE STRING QUOTED_STRING

%type <integer>      INTEGER
%type <real>         FLOAT
%type <cmd>          command
%type <cmd>          one_command
%type <cfs>          change_fmt
%type <cfs>          one_change_fmt
%type <of>           out_fmt
%type <ros>          rel_out_fmt
%type <cos>          col_out_fmt
```

```
%type <ros>            one_rel_fmt
%type <cos>            one_col_fmt
%type <strarray>       string_list
%type <str>            alias
%type <cfs>            max_min_fmt
%type <cfs>            str_change_fmt
%type <cfs>            pct_change_fmt
%type <cfs>            abs_change_fmt
%type <cfs>            any_change_fmt
%type <np>             number

%%
/*
```

*THE PARSER DESCRIPTION (read aloud to the beginning of*
*Also Sprach Zarathustra (the theme from 2001))*
*As things are discovered, they are put into the linked list structure*
*detailed in defs.h.*

```
*/

command                : one_command
            {
                if (clist == NULL)
                    clist = $1;
                else
                    printf("Bad error in the parser. \n");
            }
        pipe command one_command
            {
                struct cmd_st *p;

                if (clist != NULL) {
                    for (p=clist; p->next!=NULL; p=p->next)

                        ;
                    p->next = $2;
                }
                else
                    clist = $1;
            }
        pipe error '.'
            {
            fprintf(stderr, "Command error ");
            fprintf(stderr,"near line %d\n", control_line);
            parse_error = True;
            }
        ;

one_command                : PIPELINE alias out_fmt ' : ' change_fmt ' . '

            { $$ = build_cmd($1, $2, $3, $5); }
        ;
```

```
out_fmt                    : rel_out_fmt
               {
                       struct out_fmt_st *p;

                       p = allocate(struct out_fmt_st);
                       p->type = RELATIVE;
                       p->out_fmt.rel_fmt = $1;
                       $$ = p;
               }
           pipe col_out_fmt
               {
                       struct out_fmt_st *p;

                       p = allocate(struct out_fmt_st);
                       p->type = COLUMN;
                       p->out_fmt.col_fmt = $1;
                       $$ = p;
               }
           pipe error ' . '
               {
                       fprintf(stderr,"Output format error ");
                       fprintf(stderr,"near line %d\n",
                               control_line);
                       parse_error = True;
               }
           ;

change_fmt                     : one_change_fmt
           pipe change_fmt ' ; ' one_change_fmt
               {
               add_end(struct change_fmt_st, $1, $3, $$);
               }
           pipe error ' ; '
               {
                       fprintf(stderr,"Change format error ");
                       fprintf(stderr,"near line %d\n",
                               control_line);
                       parse_error = True;
               }
           ;

one_change_fmt                    : pct_change_fmt
           pipe abs_change_fmt
           pipe max_min_fmt
           pipe str_change_fmt
           pipe any_change_fmt
           pipe error ' . '
               {
               fprintf(stderr,"Unknown change format type ");
               fprintf(stderr,"near line %d\n", control_line);
```

```
                                    parse_error = True;
                                    }
                    ;

rel_out_fmt                          : one_rel_fmt
                    pipe rel_out_fmt one_rel_fmt
                            {
                                    add_end(struct rel_out_st, $1, $2, $$);
                            }
                    ;

col_out_fmt                          : one_col_fmt
                    pipe col_out_fmt one_col_fmt
                            {
                                    add_end(struct col_out_st, $1, $2, $$);
                            }
                    ;

one_rel_fmt                          : INTEGER STRING '%' STRING
                            { $$ = build_rel($1, $2, $4); }
                    ;

one_col_fmt                          : INTEGER '-' INTEGER STRING '%' STRING
                            { $$ = build_col($1, $3, $4, $6); }
                    ;

pct_change_fmt                       : STRING number '%'
                            { $$ = build_pct($1, $2); }
                    ;

abs_change_fmt                       : STRING number
                            { $$ = build_abs($1, $2); }
                    ;

max_min_fmt                          : STRING number number
                            { $$ = build_maxmin($1, $2, $3); }
                    ;

str_change_fmt                       : STRING string_list
                            { $$ = build_str($1, $2); nslist = 0; }
                    ;

any_change_fmt                       : STRING
                            { $$ = build_any($1); }
                    ;

string_list                          : QUOTED_STRING
                            {
                            nslist = 2;
                            $$ = (char **)xmalloc((unsigned)
                                    (nslist * sizeof(char *)));
```

```
                        $$[0] = $1;
                        $$[1] = NULL;
                        }
                pipe QUOTED_STRING ' , ' string_list
                        {
                        $3 = (char **)realloc((char *)$3, (unsigned)
                                                (++nslist * sizeof(char *)));
                        if ($3 == NULL) {
                                fprintf(stderr, "realloc failed. \n");
                                exit(1);
                        }
                        $3[nslist-2] = $1;
                        $3[nslist-1] = NULL;
                        $$ = $3;
                        }
                ;


number                  : INTEGER
                        {
                        struct number *np;

                        np = allocate(struct number);
                        np->type = INTEGER;
                        np->value.integer = $1;
                        $$ = np;
                        }
                pipe FLOAT
                        {
                        struct number *np;

                        np = allocate(struct number);
                        np->type = FLOAT;
                        np->value.real = $1;
                        $$ = np;
                        }
                ;


alias                   : '{' STRING '{'
                        {
                            $$ = $2;
                        }
                pipe empty
                        { $$ = NULL; }
                ;


empty                   : ;
```

```
/* defs.h
Structure definitions, included files needed and useful constants for
Watcher.
```

Kenneth Ingham

Copyright (C) 1987 The University of New Mexico
*/

```c
#include <stdio.h>
#include <ctype.h>

ifdef BSD
#include <strings.h>
#else
#include <string.h>
#endif

#include <signal.h>

#define False              0
#define True               1
#define SUCCESS            0
#define FAIL               1
#define EMPTY              0
#define MAX_STR            256
#define DEF_CONTROL        "watcherfile"
#define DEF_CONTROL2       "Watcherfile"
#define DEF_HISTFILE       "watcher.history"
#define VERSION            "Version 1.3"
#define MAX_NAME           16
#define MAX_VEC            100
#define STACKSIZE          256

#define ANY                2
#define PERCENT            3
#define ABSOLUTE           4
#define MAX_MIN            5
#define RELATIVE           6
#define COLUMN             7
#define KEY                9
```

```
/*
Below lie the structure definitions for all of the linked lists used
in watcher.
*/
```

```c
/* we start easy. a number is either an int or a float... */
struct number {
        int type;
        union {
               float real;
               int integer;
        } value;
};
```

```
/*
what a column output format entry looks like:
*/
struct col_out_st {
        char *name;                 /* name of output field */

        int start;                  /* where it starts... */
        int end;                    /* ... and ends */
        int type;                   /* what type of data to find there */

        struct col_out_st *next;    /* and the next in the list */

};


/*
and a relative output format...
*/
struct rel_out_st {

        char *name;                 /* name of output field */

        int field;                  /* Which field to look in for it */

        int type;                   /* what type of data to find there */

        struct rel_out_st *next;    /* and the next in the list */

};


/*
types of change formats; all joined in a union later.
*/
struct max_min_st {
        double max;                 /* max allowable value... */

        double min;                 /* ...and the min */
};

union fmt_u {
        float percent;              /* percent change */

        double abs_amount;          /* absolute change */

        struct max_min_st max_min;  /* max and min */

        char **str_value;           /* array of values for what the
                                       string should be; terminated
                                       by a NULL pointer */
};
```

```
struct chg_fmt_st {
        int type;
        union fmt_u fmt;
};

/*
the actual structure describing how things are allowed to change.
*/
struct change_fmt_st {
        char *name;                   /* name of the field this pertains to */
        struct chg_fmt_st fmt;        /* the format, depending on type */

        struct change_fmt_st *next;   /* and of course the next in the list */

};

/*
for the various types of output formats:
*/
union out_fmt_u {
        struct rel_out_st *rel_fmt;   /* a relative output format */

        struct col_out_st *col_fmt;   /* or one that uses column format */

};

struct out_fmt_st {
        int type;
        union out_fmt_u out_fmt;
};
```

/*
what we are all about: the command structure. Here we bring it all
together and have something to work with (luckily the subroutines are

also set up in a similar heirarchy and we can pass various parts of
the linked lists to them and they don't care about the "upper" parts.

*/

```
struct cmd_st {
        char *pipeline;                     /* the pipeline to execute */

        char *alias;                        /* a name to use when referring to it */

        struct out_fmt_st *out_fmt;         /* the output format */

        struct out_fmt_st *key;             /* what to key on for btwn run cmps */

        struct change_fmt_st *change_fmt;   /* the things to watch for changes */
```

```
        struct cmd_st *next;                    /* and of course the next in the list */

};

/*
now we get into the structures for the history linked list...
*/

/*
a way of storing any data type:
*/
union everything_u {
        char *string, character;
        int integer;
        float real;
};

struct everything {
        int type;
        union everything_u data;
};

/*
which is used here where we hold the value for a specified key value
from the previous output.
*/
struct val_st {
        char *name;                 /* output field name */

        struct everything val;      /* ... the data (wow!) */

        struct val_st *next;        /* and where would we be without the next one */

};

/*
for each line in the output of a command, we grab the key and store

all of the values obtained from the line. Here is how it is done.
*/
struct key_st {
        char *key_value;            /* value for the key (could you guess) */

        struct val_st *vals;        /* the various interesting parts of the line */

        struct key_st *next;        /* and of course the next one */

};
```

```
/*
finally we come to the reason for all of the above structures. This is
how previous commands are stored once they have been read in from the

history file.
*/
struct old_cmd_st {
        char *pipeline;                 /* the pipeline executed */

        struct key_st *keys;            /* the keys and their useful parts */

        struct old_cmd_st *next;        /* and the next pipeline... */

};

char *xmalloc(), *realloc(), *strsave(), *strnsave();
char *get_rel_field(), *get_col_field();
double atof();
struct old_cmd_st *find_cmd_prev();

/* Berkeley vs System V differences */
#ifdef SYSV
#define index           strchr
#define rindex           strrchr
#endif

#define allocate(size)          ((size *)xmalloc(sizeof(size)))


/*
do_args: parse the command line arguments and set variables related to

them.

See main for description of flags.

Kenneth Ingham

Copyright (C) 1987 The University of New Mexico
*/

#include "defs.h"

do_args(argc, argv)
int argc;
char *argv[];
{
        extern int pflag, cflag, vflag, nflag, lexverbose;
        extern char *controlname, *histfilename, *myname;
```

```
register int i;
char *slash;

/* remember who we are */
myname = argv[0];
/* if we have a pathname for a name, keep only the last component */

if ((slash = rindex(myname, '/')) != NULL)
        myname = slash+1;

/* defaults */
pflag = False; cflag = False; vflag = False; nflag = False;
lexverbose = False;
histfilename = DEF_HISTFILE;

for (i=1; i<argc; i++) {

        if (argv[i][0] == '-') {
                switch(argv[i][1]) {
                case 'v':                       /* verbose */
                        vflag = True;
                        break;
                case 'p':                       /* pretty-print control file */

                        pflag = True;
                        break;
                case 'h':                       /* specify history file */

                        i = getargv(&histfilename, argv, i,
                        "history file name");
                        break;
                case 'f':                       /* specify control file */

                        i = getargv(&controlname, argv, i,
                        "control file name");
                        cflag = True;
                        break;
                case 'n':                       /* no history */

                        nflag = True;
                        break;
                default:
                        fprintf(stderr, "Unknown flag '%s'\n", argv[i]);

                        exit(1);
                }
        }
}
if (pflag && vflag)
        lexverbose = True;
}
```

```
/*
doit: here is where the real purpose of the program is actually
carried out.

        for each command, run it and look for problems.
        write info from this run to the history file.

Kenneth Ingham

Copyright (C) 1987 The University of New Mexico
*/

#include "defs.h"

doit(hf)
FILE *hf;
{
        extern struct cmd_st *clist;
        extern int vflag, nflag;
        extern int cmd_ok;
        extern int errno;
        extern char *sys_errlist[];

        char line[MAX_STR];
        struct cmd_st *p;
        struct old_cmd_st *prev_results, *find_cmd_prev();
        FILE *ps, *popen();

        /* run commands */
        for (p=clist; p != NULL; p=p->next) {
            cmd_ok = True;
            if (vflag)
                printf("Executing: '%s'\n\n", p->pipeline);

            if ( ! nflag ) {
                /* dealing with the history file... */
                if (p->key != NULL && ! nflag)
                    fprintf(hf, "%s\n", p->pipeline);
                /* get prev results for comparison */
                prev_results = find_cmd_prev(p->pipeline);
            }
            else
                prev_results = NULL;

            if ((ps = popen(p->pipeline, "r")) == NULL) {
                fprintf(stderr, "Unable to popen '%s': %s\n",
                        p->pipeline, sys_errlist[errno]);
                fprintf(stderr, "Going to next pipeline.\n");
                continue;
            }
```

```
        while (fgets(line, MAX_STR, ps) != NULL) {
                line[strlen(line)-1] = '\0'; /* remove newline */
                if (vflag)
                        printf(" Read: '%s'\n",line);
                checkline(p, line, prev_results, hf);
                errno = 0;
        }

        if (errno)
                fprintf(stderr, "Error reading from '%s': %s\n",

                        p->pipeline, sys_errlist[errno]);

        (void) pclose(ps);
        if (!cmd_ok)
                printf("\n");
        }
}


/*
extern: external variable declarations for all of the program.
Beware though that many of the variables that the parser uses are
actually externs also due to the way variables are declared for use
with yacc.

Kenneth Ingham

Copyright (C) 1987 The University of New Mexico
*/

#include "defs.h"
#include "y.tab.h"

struct cmd_st *clist = NULL;
struct old_cmd_st *chead = NULL;

int parse_error = False;

int pflag, cflag, vflag, nflag;
int lexverbose;
char *histfilename;
char *controlname;
int line_ok;
int cmd_ok;
int control_line = 1;
char *myname;

struct out_fmt_st *key = NULL;
```

```
/*
find_of: find the output format corresponding for the field whose
name we are given.

Kenneth Ingham

Copyright (C) 1987 The University of New Mexico
*/

#include "defs.h"

find_of(name, of_head, of)
struct out_fmt_st *of_head, *of;
char *name;
{
        struct rel_out_st *rf;
        struct col_out_st *cf;

        of->type = of_head->type;
        switch(of_head->type) {
            case RELATIVE:
                for (rf=of_head->out_fmt.rcl_fmt; rf; rf=rf->next)
                    if (strcmp(name, rf->name) == 0) {
                            of->out_fmt.rel_fmt = rf;
                            return True;

                    }
                break;
            case COLUMN:
                for (cf=of_head->out_fmt.col_fmt; cf; cf=cf->next)
                    if (strcmp(name, cf->name) == 0) {
                            of->out_fmt.col_fmt = cf;
                            return True;

                    }
                break;
            default:
                fprintf(stderr, "internal error; unknown type %d",
                    of_head->type);
                fprintf(stderr, " in find_of\n");
                exit(1);
        }

        return False;
}




/*
find_cmd_prev: find the previous results for this command (if any). If
there is no match, then we return NULL by falling through the loop.
```

Kenneth Ingham

Copyright (C) 1987 The University of New Mexico
*/

**#include** "defs.h"

**struct** old_cmd_st *
find_cmd_prev(pipeline)
**char** *pipeline;
{
        **extern struct** old_cmd_st *chead;
        **struct** old_cmd_st *cp;

        cp = chead;
        **while** (cp != NULL && strcmp(pipeline, cp->pipeline) != 0)

            cp = cp->next;

        **return** cp;
}


/*
find_prev_value: given an old command structure, look through the
prior output for the output for name of type type. Return it in the
struct pointed to by value or NULL if not found.

Kenneth Ingham

Copyright (C) 1987 The University of New Mexico
*/

**#include** "defs.h"

find_prev_value(cmd, field_name, key_val, value)
**struct** old_cmd_st *cmd;
**char** *field_name, *key_val;
**struct** everything **value;
{
        **struct** val_st *vp;
        **struct** key_st *kp;

        *value = NULL;

        /* is there anything to look for a value for? */
        **if** (cmd == NULL pipepipe cmd->keys == NULL)
            **return**;

```
        /* find the correct key */
        kp = cmd->keys;
        while (kp != NULL && strcmp(kp->key_value, key_val) != 0)

                kp = kp->next;

        /* was a keyword and value found? */
        if (kp == NULL pipepipe kp->vals == NULL)
                return;

        /* find the value under the keyword */

        vp = kp->vals;
        while (vp != NULL && strcmp(vp->name, field_name) != 0)

                vp = vp->next;

        *value = &(vp->val);
}


/*
get_col_field: we have a column output format and want a certain
part of it. Place the it in 'value' if it exists and return a
pointer to the string. If there are problems place a null terminated
zero length string in 'value' and return NULL as an error condition.

Kenneth Ingham

Copyright (C) 1987 The University of New Mexico
*/

#include "defs.h"
char *
get_col_field(line, start, end, value)
char *line, *value;
int start, end;
{
        int len;

        value[0] = '\0';
        len = strlen(line);

        /* error checking */
        if (start > len pipepipe end > len) {
                fprintf(stderr,"'%s' has %d columns. Specified were %d to %d\n"

                        line, len, start, start);
                return NULL;
        }
```

```
        len = end - start + 1;
        strncpy(value, &line[start-1], len)[len] = '\0';

        return value;
}



/*
get_rel_field: we have a relative output format and want a certain
field from it. Place the field in 'value' if it exists and return a
pointer to the string. If there are problems place a null terminated
zero length string in 'value' and return NULL as an error condition.

Kenneth Ingham

Copyright (C) 1987 The University of New Mexico
*/

#include "defs.h"

char *
get_rel_field(line, field, value)
char *line, *value;
int field;
{
        int i;
        int nfields;
        char *vec[MAX_VEC];

        value[0] = '\0';

        /* break up the line */
        nfields = line_to_vec(line, vec, " \t");

        /* error checking */
        if (nfields <= 0) {
            fprintf(stderr, "'%s' didn't break up into fields.\n",line);

            return NULL;
        }
        if (nfields < field) {
            fprintf(stderr, "Warning: '%s' has only %d fields, not %d\n",
                line, nfields, field);
            return NULL;
        }

        (void) strcpy(value, vec[field-1]);

        for (i=0; i<nfields; i++)
            free(vec[i]);
```

```
        return value;
}



/*
getargv: get a value from argv, whether it is immediately following
the flag or is the next argument. Complain if not found and exit.

Kenneth Ingham

Copyright (C) 1987 The University of New Mexico
*/

#include "defs.h"

getargv(what, argv, i, err)
char **what, *argv[], *err;
int i;
{
        if (argv[i][2])
                *what = strsave(&argv[i][2]);
        else {
            if (argv[++i])
                    *what = strsave(argv[i]);
            else {
                    fprintf(stderr,"Missing %s!\n", err);
                    exit(1);
            }
        }
        return i;
}



/*
hist_cmd: a command has been read from the history file. Do the
necessary list-building activities for a new command.

Kenneth Ingham

Copyright (C) 1988 The University of New Mexico
*/

#include "defs.h"

hist_cmd(line, cmd_head, cmd_ptr, key_ptr, value_ptr)
char *line;
struct old_cmd_st **cmd_head, **cmd_ptr;
struct key_st **key_ptr;
```

```
struct val_st **value_ptr;
{
        /* is this the first? */
        if (*cmd_head == NULL) {
            *cmd_head = *cmd_ptr = allocate(struct old_cmd_st);
        }
        else {
            (*cmd_ptr)->next = allocate(struct old_cmd_st);
            *cmd_ptr = (*cmd_ptr)->next;
        }

        (*cmd_ptr)->keys = NULL;
        (*cmd_ptr)->next = NULL;
        (*cmd_ptr)->pipeline = strsave(line);
        (*cmd_ptr)->next = NULL;
        *key_ptr == NULL;
        *value_ptr == NULL;
}
```

```
/*
hist_key: a key has been found in the history file. After error
checking, set up the list structure for the key.

Kenneth Ingham

Copyright (C) The University of New Mexico
*/

#include "defs.h"

hist_key(line, cmd_ptr, key_ptr, value_ptr)
char *line;
struct old_cmd_st **cmd_ptr;
struct key_st **key_ptr;
struct val_st **value_ptr;
{
        if (*cmd_ptr == NULL) {
            printf("Bad history file: keyword found before pipeline. \n");

            printf("Ignoring history file. \n");
            return FAIL;
        }

        /* is this the first key for this command? */
        if ((*cmd_ptr)->keys == NULL) {
            (*cmd_ptr)->keys = allocate(struct key_st);
            *key_ptr = (*cmd_ptr)->keys;
        }
```

```
else {
        (*key_ptr)->next = allocate(struct key_st);
        *key_ptr = (*key_ptr)->next;
}

(*key_ptr)->next = NULL;
(*key_ptr)->vals = NULL;
(*key_ptr)->key_value = strsave(&line[1]);
*value_ptr = NULL;

return SUCCESS;
}
```

```
/*
hist_value: a value has been found in the history file. Insert it
into the list.

Kenneth Ingham

Copyright (C) 1988 The University of New Mexico
*/

#include "defs.h"
#include "y.tab.h"

hist_value(line, key_ptr, value_ptr)
char *line;
struct key_st **key_ptr;
struct val_st **value_ptr;
{
        unsigned int len;
        char *sp, *strnsave();

        /* consistency check */
        if (*key_ptr == NULL) {
            printf("Bad history file: value found before keyword.\n");

            printf("Ignoring history file.\n");
            return FAIL;
        }

        /* is this the first value for this key? */
        if ((*key_ptr)->vals == NULL) {
            (*key_ptr)->vals = allocate(struct val_st);
            *value_ptr = (*key_ptr)->vals;
        }
        else {
            (*value_ptr)->next = allocate(struct val_st);
            *value_ptr = (*value_ptr)->next;
        }
```

```
(*value_ptr)->next = NULL;

/*
find the space which separates the name from the type, then

get the name
*/
sp = index(&line[2], ' ');
if (sp == NULL) {
    printf("Garbled history file; no name-type sep. \n");

    printf("Ignoring history file. \n");
    return FAIL;
}
len = sp - &line[2];
(*value_ptr)->name = strnsave(&line[2], len);
(*value_ptr)->name[len] = '\0';

sp++; /* sp now points at the type, sp+2 is the first char of val */

if (!*(sp+1) pipepipe !*(sp+2)) {
    printf("Garbled history file; no value. \n");
    printf("Ignoring history file. \n");
    return FAIL;
}

switch (*sp) {
    case 's':
        (*value_ptr)->val.type = STRING;
        (*value_ptr)->val.data.string = strsave(sp+2);
        break;
    case 'f':
        (*value_ptr)->val.type = FLOAT;
        (*value_ptr)->val.data.real = atof(sp+2);
        break;
    case 'd':
        (*value_ptr)->val.type = INTEGER;
        (*value_ptr)->val.data.integer = atoi(sp+2);
        break;
    default:
        /* bad condition */
        printf("Unknown data type in history file. \n")

        printf("Offending line: %s\n",line);
        printf("Ignoring history file. \n");
        return FAIL;
        break;
}
```

```
        return SUCCESS;
}



/*
init_sigs: take care of setting up the signal handling.

Kenneth Ingham

Copyright (C) 1987 The University of New Mexico
*/

#include "defs.h"

init_sigs()
{
        extern int vflag;
        int exit(), baderr();

        (void) signal(SIGINT, exit);
        (void) signal(SIGHUP, exit);

        /*
        if verbose is on, let's leave a core dump behind for
        debugging
        */
        if (!vflag) {
                (void) signal(SIGQUIT, baderr);
                (void) signal(SIGSEGV, baderr);
                (void) signal(SIGBUS, baderr);
                (void) signal(SIGFPE, baderr);
                (void) signal(SIGILL, baderr);
        }
}



/*
line_to_vec: take a string and separate it into a vector of strings,
        splitting it at characters which are supplied in 'splits'.
        Ignore any 'splits' at the beginning. Multiple 'splits' are
        condensed into one. Splits are discarded.

Assumptions:
        line is null terminated.
        no single word is longer than MAX_STR.

Arguments:
        line: line to split.
        vec: split line.
        splits: array of characters on which to split. Null terminated.
```

Local variables:
> name: current entry in the vector we are building.
> word: pointer into name.

Returns:
> The number of vectors created.
> The argument vec is left with a NULL pointer after the last word.

Kenneth Ingham

Copyright (C) 1987 The University of New Mexico
*/

```c
#include "defs.h"

line_to_vec(line, vec, splits)
char *line, *vec[], *splits;
{
        register int i, v, j;
        int n;
        char word[MAX_STR];

        if (line == NULL pipepipe line[0] == '\0')
                return 0;

        /* skip any splits in the beginning */
        for (i=0; line[i] && index(splits, line[i]) != 0; i++)
                ;

        j = 0;
        v = 0;
        n = 0;
        while (line[i]) {
                if (index(splits, line[i]) != 0) { /* found the end of a word */

                        word[j] = '\0';
                        vec[v] = strsave(word);
                        j = 0;
                        v++;
                        n++;
                        i++;
                        for ( ; line[i] && index(splits, line[i]) != 0; i++)
                                ;
                }
                else
                        word[j++] = line[i++];
        }

        /* deal with the last word if the line didn't end in a "split". */
```

```
    if (index(splits, line[i]) != 0) {
        word[j] = '\0';
        vec[v] = strsave(word);
        n++;
    }

    return n;
}
```

```
/*
main: main routine for the watcher program.

read from a file describing commands (pipelines) to execute, formats of

    the output, max changes allowed (% or absolute), and max & min

    values for various fields.
problems noticed are reported.
as a side effect, be able to pretty print the description file
    (originally used to verify parsing).

outline of program:
    parse control file and build data structures.
    run each pipeline and compare output to previous output (only

        save relevant fields; save directory is either default
        or command line specified; no previous file or format
        changed (ie we are watching different or new fields) we
        create new file and next time we do compare).
    differences that are not allowable are reported.

Usage of program:
    watcher [-p] [-v] [-h histfile] [-f controlfile] [-n]

    -p : pretty print control file as a verification of parse
        (default no pretty print). This option prevents
        processing of control file.
    -v : be verbose when doing work; useful for debugging.
        Shows what was read from processes, or if used in
        conjunction with -p shows what the lexical analyzer
        returned.
    -h : file in which to save output for future compare (default
        ./watcher.history).
    -f : controlfile to use (default ./watcherfile or ./Watcherfile).
    -n : turn off 'history' stuff, if set.
```

Note that the basic data structures are all linear linked lists, with many items in the list being heads of other lists. When problems occur, get out the pencil and paper and start drawing the lists.

Kenneth Ingham

```c
#include "defs.h"

main(argc, argv)
int argc;
char *argv[];
{
        extern int parse_error;
        extern struct cmd_st *clist;
        extern int pflag, nflag;
        extern char *myname, *histfilename;
        extern int errno;
        extern char *sys_errlist[];
        FILE *hf;

        do_args(argc, argv);
        init_sigs();
        open_cf();

        if (yyparse() == 1 pipepipe parse_error) {
            fprintf(stderr, "%s: parse error in control file.\n", myname);

            exit(1);
        }

        if (clist == NULL) {
            fprintf(stderr, "No command list to execute!\n");
            exit(1);
        }

        if (pflag)
            pp(clist);
        else {
            if (! nflag) {
                read_hist();
                hf = fopen(histfilename, "w");
                if (hf == NULL) {
                    fprintf(stderr, "Unable to open '%s': %s\n",

                        histfilename, sys_errlist[errno]);
                    exit(1);
                }
            }
            doit(hf);
        }
}
```

```
/*
maxmin_check: verify that the value is between min and max.

Kenneth Ingham

Copyright (C) 1988 The University of New Mexico
*/

#include "defs.h"
#include "y.tab.h"

maxmin_check(current, max, min, cmd, name, line)
char *current;
double max, min;
char *cmd, *name, *line;
{
        extern int line_ok, cmd_ok;
        double value;

        value = atof(current);

        if (value > max pipeline value < min) {
            if (line_ok) {
                printf("%s has a ", cmd);
                printf("max/min value out of range: \n");
                printf("%s\n",line);
            }
            else {
                printf("Also, it has a ");
                printf("max/min value out of range: \n");
            }
            printf("where %s = %.2f; ", name, value);
            printf("valid range %.2f to %.2f.\n", min, max);
            line_ok = False;
        }
}


/*
open_cf: open the control file. It is either specified on the
command line or DEF_CONTROL or DEF_CONTROL2.

To make life easier dealing with lex, the control file is opened as
stdin.

Kenneth Ingham

Copyright (C) 1987 The University of New Mexico
*/
```

```
#include "defs.h"

open_cf()
{
        extern char *controlname;
        extern int cflag;
        extern int errno;
        extern char *sys_errlist[];
        FILE *cf;

        if (cflag) { /* specified control file */
                cf = freopen(controlname, "r", stdin);
                if (cf == NULL) {
                        fprintf(stderr, "Unable to open '%s': %s\n",
                                controlname, sys_errlist[errno]);
                        exit(1);
                }
        }
        else { /* try defaults */
                if ((cf = freopen(DEF_CONTROL, "r", stdin)) == NULL) { /* #1 */

                        if ((cf = freopen(DEF_CONTROL2, "r", stdin)) == NULL) { /* #2 */

                                fprintf(stderr, "Unable to open %s or %s: %s\n",
                                        DEF_CONTROL, DEF_CONTROL2,
                                        sys_errlist[errno]);
                                exit(1);
                        }
                        /* if we're here #2 must have worked */
                        controlname = DEF_CONTROL2;
                }
                else
                        /* if we're here #1 must have worked */
                        controlname = DEF_CONTROL;
        }
}


/*
open_hf: open the history file for reading, taking care of the errors
that can occur.

Note that a missing history file is not an error. We just don't do
anything that uses previous values.

Copyright (C) 1987 The University of New Mexico
*/

#include "defs.h"
#include <errno.h>
```

```
FILE *
open_hf()
{
        extern int vflag;
        extern char *histfilename;
        extern int errno;
        extern char *sys_errlist[];
        extern struct old_cmd_st *chead;

        FILE *hf;

        if (vflag)
            printf("Using %s for historyfile\n", histfilename);

        hf = fopen(histfilename, "r");
        if (hf == NULL) {
            if (errno == ENOENT) {
                if (vflag)
                    printf("This is a first run. \n");
            }
            else { /* some other error */
                fprintf(stderr, "Warning. ");
                fprintf(stderr, "unable to open history file. \n");
                fprintf(stderr, "%s: %s\n", histfilename,
                    sys_errlist[errno]);
                fprintf(stderr, "Ignoring history file. \n\n");
            }
            chead = NULL;
            return NULL;
        }

        return hf;
}



/*
pct_check: verify that the value has not changed more than the
allowed percentage.

Kenneth Ingham

Copyright (C) 1988 The University of New Mexico
*/

#include "defs.h"

pct_check(current, prev_val, percent, cmd, name, line)
char *current;
double percent;
```

```
struct everything *prev_val;
char *cmd, *name, *line;
{
        extern int line_ok, cmd_ok;
        double change, previous, value;
        double to_double();

        previous = to_double(prev_val);
        value = atof(current);

        if (value == 0) /* avoid divide by 0 */
            return;

        change = (value - previous) / value;
        if (change > percent) {
            if (line_ok) {
                printf("%s had ", cmd);
                printf("%s change by more than %.2f percent.\n",

                    name, percent*100);
                printf("%s\n",line);
            }
            else {
                printf("Also, it had ");
                printf("%s change by more than %.2f percent.\n",

                    name, percent*100);
            }
            printf("Previous value %.2f; ", previous);
            printf("current value %.2f.\n", value);
            line_ok = False;
        }
}


/*
pp: pretty print the command structure.

Kenneth Ingham

Copyright (C) 1987 The University of New Mexico
*/

#include "defs.h"

pp(clist)
struct cmd_st *clist;
{
        extern char *histfilename;
        extern char *controlname;
        extern char *myname;
```

```
        printf("%s %s\n", myname, VERSION);
        printf("History file name: %s\n", histfilename);
        printf("Control file name: %s\n", controlname);
        printf("\n\n");

        while (clist != NULL) {
                printf(" ( %s ) ", clist->pipeline);
                if (clist->alias[0])
                        printf(" { '%s' }\n", clist->alias);
                else
                        printf("\n");
                pp_out(clist->out_fmt);
                printf(" : \n");
                pp_change(clist->change_fmt);
                clist = clist->next;
        }
}


/*
pp_change: pretty print the change format.

Kenneth Ingham

Copyright (C) 1987 The University of New Mexico
*/

#include "defs.h"
#include "y.tab.h"

pp_change(cf)
struct change_fmt_st *cf;
{
        int i;

        while (cf != NULL) {
                switch(cf->fmt.type) {
                    case PERCENT:
                        printf("\t\t%s %5.2f %%", cf->name,
                            cf->fmt.fmt.percent*100);
                        break;
                    case ABSOLUTE:
                        printf("\t\t%s %6.2f", cf->name,
                            cf->fmt.fmt.abs_amount);
                        break;
                    case MAX_MIN:
                        printf("\t\t%s %6.2f %6.2f", cf->name,
                            cf->fmt.fmt.max_min.min,
                            cf->fmt.fmt.max_min.max);
                        break;
```

```
            case STRING:
                    printf("\t\t%s", cf->name);
                    printf(" \"%s\"", cf->fmt.fmt.str_value[0]);
                    for (i=1; cf->fmt.fmt.str_value[i]; i++)
                            printf(", \"%s\"",
                                    cf->fmt.fmt.str_value[i]);
                    break;
            case ANY:
                    printf("\t\t%s", cf->name);
                    break;
            default:
                    printf("Impossible change format type: %d\n",

                            cf->fmt.type);
                    break;
            }
            if (cf->next != NULL)
                    printf(" ; \n");
            else
                    printf(" . \n");
            cf = cf->next;
        }
}


/*
pp_out: pretty print the output of command structure.

Kenneth Ingham

Copyright (C) 1987 The University of New Mexico
*/

#include "defs.h"
#include "y.tab.h"

pp_out(of)
struct out_fmt_st *of;
{
        struct rel_out_st *rp;
        struct col_out_st *cp;
        char tchar();

        switch(of->type) {
            case RELATIVE:
                    rp = of->out_fmt.rel_fmt;
                    while (rp != NULL) {
                            printf(" %d %s %%%c", rp->field, rp->name,
                                    tchar(rp->type));
```

```
                    rp = rp->next;
            }
            break;
    case COLUMN:
            cp = of->out_fmt.col_fmt;
            while (cp != NULL) {
                    printf(" %d-%d %s %%c", cp->start, cp->end,

                            cp->name, tchar(cp->type));
                    cp = cp->next;
            }
            break;
    default:
            fprintf(stderr, "Impossible value for output ");

            fprintf(stderr, "format. type: %d\n", of->type);
            break;
        }
}
```

```
/*
```
read_hist: open the file containing the results of our last run. If
it is not there then we assume that this is a first run and set the
head of the list to NULL. Otherwise, we read the results of the previous

run into a mess of a data structure for later use in comparisons.

Assumed format of history file:

command
\tkey
\t\tname type value

with the following definitions:
        command: pipeline that was executed
        key: vlue of key on line
        name: output field name
        type: field name (same as defined in output format)
        value: what was in the field.

We create a linked list of linked lists of linked lists. An improvement

would be to change to a tree of some sort to speed up searches.

Kenneth Ingham

Copyright (C) 1987 The University of New Mexico
```
*/
```

```c
#include "defs.h"
#include "y.tab.h"
#include <sys/errno.h>

read_hist()
{
        extern struct old_cmd_st *chead;
        extern int errno;
        extern char *sys_errlist[];
        extern char *histfilename;
        FILE *hf;
        char line[MAX_STR];
        struct old_cmd_st *cp;
        struct val_st *vp;
        struct key_st *kp;
        FILE *open_hf();

        if ((hf = open_hf()) == NULL)
            return; /* errors are dealt with in open_hf */

        chead = NULL; cp = NULL; kp = NULL;
        while (fgets(line, MAX_STR, hf) != NULL) {
            line[strlen(line)-1] = '\0'; /* kill trailing newline */

            if (line[0] != '\t') /* command */
                hist_cmd(line, &chead, &cp, &kp, &vp);
            else if (line[0] == '\t' && line[1] != '\t') { /* key */
                if (hist_key(line, &cp, &kp, &vp) == FAIL) {
                    chead = NULL;
                    return;
                }
            }
            else if (line[0] == '\t' && line[1] == '\t') { /* values */

                if (hist_value(line, &kp, &vp) == FAIL) {
                    chead = NULL;
                    return;
                }
            }
            errno = 0;
        }

        if (errno) {
            fprintf(stderr, "Warning: error reading %s: %s\n",
                histfilename, sys_errlist[errno]);
            fprintf(stderr, "Ignoring history file.\n\n");
            chead = NULL;
        }

        (void) fclose(hf);
}
```

```
/*
save_key: save the key for this line in the history file so that
we can use it next run.

Assume that the keyword file is opened and that the pipeline has
already been placed in the file. We place the data in the file in
the following format:

pipeline
\tkey_value
\t\tname value
 .
 .
 .


Side effect: return the actual key value for other parts of the
program to use.

Kenneth Ingham

Copyright (C) 1987 The University of New Mexico
*/
```

**#include** "def s. h"

```
save_key(cmd, line, key_val, hf)
```
**struct** cmd_st *cmd;
**char** *line, *key_val;
FILE *hf;
{
   **extern int** vflag;

   **if** (cmd->key == NULL) { /* *no key; no reason to save.* */
     **if** (vflag)
      printf("%s has no key f ield. \n",cmd->pipeline);

     **return;**
   }

   **switch** (cmd->out_fmt->type) {
    **case** RELATIVE:
      (**void**) get_rel_field(line,
        cmd->key->out_fmt.rel_fmt->field,
        key_val);
      **break;**
    **case** COLUMN:
      (**void**) get_col_field(line,
        cmd->key->out_fmt.col_fmt->start,
        cmd->key->out_fmt.col_fmt->end, key_val);
      **break;**
   }

```
    if (!key_val[0]) {
        if (vflag)
            printf("the key field for %s is empty\n",cmd->pipeline);

        return;
    }
    fprintf(hf, "\t%s\n",key_val);
}


/*
str_check: check a string value and make sure it is in the list of
acceptable values.

Kenneth Ingham

Copyright (C) 1988 The University of New Mexico
*/

#include "defs.h"

str_check(value, acceptable, cmd, name, line)
char *value, **acceptable;
char *cmd, *name, *line;
{
        extern int line_ok;
        int ok, i;

        ok = False;

        for (i=0; acceptable[i]; i++) {
            if (strcmp(acceptable[i], value) == 0) {
                ok = True;
                break;
            }
        }

        if (!ok) {
            if (line_ok) {
                printf("%s has a string ", cmd);
                printf("value which is not valid: \n");
                printf("%s\n",line);
            }
            else {
                printf("Also, it has a string ");
                printf("value which is not valid: \n");
            }

            printf("where %s = '%s'; Should be '%s'", name, value,
```

```
                    acceptable[0]);
            for (i=1; acceptable[i]; i++)
                printf(" or '%s'",acceptable[i]);
            printf("\n");
            line_ok = False;
        }
}
```

```
/*
strsave: save a string in a malloc'd area. Return a pointer to the
string.

Kenneth Ingham

Copyright (C) The University of New Mexico
*/
```

```
#include "defs.h"

char *
strsave(s)
char *s;
{
        return strcpy(xmalloc((unsigned)strlen(s)+1), s);
}
```

```
/*
note that in strnsave we allocate enough space to put a null at the
end.
*/
char *
strnsave(s,n)
char *s;
unsigned int n;
{
        return strncpy(xmalloc(n+1), s, (int)n);
}
```

```
/*
tchar: convert from an output format type back to the character
which represents it.

Kenneth Ingham

Copyright (C) 1988 The University of New Mexico
*/
```

```
#include "defs.h"
#include "y.tab.h"

/*
structure used to map types back to characters for printing out
*/
struct type_char {
        int type;
        char c;
};

char
tchar(type)
int type;
{
        int i;
        static struct type_char types[] = {
              { STRING,                 's'},
              { INTEGER,                'd'},
              { FLOAT,                  'f'},
              { KEY,                    'k'},
              { 0,                      '\0'}
        };

        for (i=0; types[i].type && types[i].type != type; i++)
              ;

        if (types[i].type == NULL) {
              fprintf(stderr, "Internal error, unknown output format ");

              fprintf(stderr, "type %d\n", type);
              exit(1);
        }

        return types[i].c;
}


/*
to_double: convert a struct anything to a double, no matter what type

it is currently.

I'm not completely happy with this; should make better use of
the info we are provided about the type of any instead of calling
this routine.

Kenneth Ingham
*/
```

```
#include "defs.h"
#include "y.tab.h"

double
to_double(any)
struct everything *any;
{
        switch (any->type) {
            case STRING:
                    return (double)atof(any->data.string);
            case FLOAT:
                    return any->data.real;
            case INTEGER:
                    return (double)any->data.integer;
            default:
                    fprintf(stderr, "Unable to convert type %d",any->type);

                    fprintf(stderr, " to double.\n");
                    exit(1);
        }
        /*NOTREACHED*/
}
```

```
/*
to_string: convert a struct anything to a string, no matter what type

it is currently.

I'm not completely happy with this; should make better use of
the info we are provided about the type of any instead of calling
this routine.

Note that we assume that a real or integer will fit in a string
of length MAX_STR.

Note also that we return a pointer to a static area.

Kenneth Ingham
*/

#include "defs.h"
#include "y.tab.h"

char *
to_string(any)
struct everything *any;
{
        static char rvalue[MAX_STR];
```

```
        switch (any->type) {
            case STRING:
                return any->data.string;
            case FLOAT:
                sprintf(rvalue, "%f", any->data.real);
                return rvalue;
            case INTEGER:
                sprintf(rvalue, "%d", any->data.integer);
                return rvalue;
            default:
                fprintf(stderr, "Unable to convert type %d",any->type);
                fprintf(stderr, " to string. \n");
                exit(1);
        }
        /*NOTREACHED*/
}


/*
xmalloc is just a call to malloc with error checking.

Kenneth Ingham

Copyright (C) 1989 The University of New Mexico
*/

#include "defs.h"

char *
xmalloc(size)
unsigned size;
{
        char *cp, *malloc();

        cp = malloc(size);

        if (cp == NULL) {
            fprintf(stderr,"malloc died. ");
            exit(1);
        }

        return cp;
}


/*
yyerror: print out the errors for the parser. To be helpful, we
print the line number in the control file where the problem occurred.
```

Kenneth Ingham

Copyright (C) 1987 The University of New Mexico
*/

**#include** "defs.h"

```
yyerror(s)
char *s;
{
        extern int control_line;

        fprintf(stderr,"%s on or near line %d\n", s, control_line);
}
```

%{
/*

yylex.l: lex version of the lexical analyzer for watcher.

Kenneth Ingham

Copyright (C) 1989 The University of New Mexico
*/

**#include** "defs.h"
**#include** "y.tab.h"

**extern int** lexverbose;
**extern int** control_line;
%}

%%

```
"."                     return '.';
","                     return ',';
";"                     return ';';
":"                     return ':';
"%"                     return '%';
"-"                     return '-';
"+"                     return '+';
"{"                     return '{';
"}"                     roturn '}';

\([^)]*\)          {       /* pipeline */
                        /* start at 1 due to ( */
                        yylval.str = strnsave(&yytext[1], yyleng-2);
                        yylval.str[yyleng-2] = '\0';
```

```
                    if (lexverbose)
                        printf("pipeline; '%s'\n", yylval.str);
                    return PIPELINE;
            }

[0-9]*\.[0-9]+          {           /* float */
                    /*
                    note a float cannot end in a . since we also
                    end entries with '.' and we couldn't tell
                    them apart (unless we used lookahead)
                    */

                    yylval.real = (float) atof(yytext);
                    if (lexverbose)
                        printf("float: '%f'\n", yylval.real);
                    return FLOAT;
            }

[0-9]+          {           /* integer */
                    yylval.integer = atoi(yytext);
                    if (lexverbose)
                        printf("integer: '%d'\n", yylval.integer);
                    return INTEGER;
            }

('[^']*')pipe(\"[^\"]*\")           {           /* string in 's or "s */

                    /* copy, *except* for 's */
                    yylval.str =strnsave(&yytext[1], yyleng-2);
                    yylval.str[yyleng-2] = '\0';

                    if (lexverbose)
                        printf("string in %cs: '%s'\n", yytext[0],
                        yylval.str);

                    if (yytext[0] == '"')
                        return QUOTED_STRING;
                    else /* string is in 's */
                        return STRING;
            }

[a-zA-Z_][a-zA-Z_0-9]*           {/* string */
                    yylval.str = strsave(yytext);

                    if (lexverbose)
                        printf("string: '%s'\n", yytext);

                    return STRING;
            }
```

```
[\t]+            ; /* white space - ignored */

\n              { control_line++; } /* newline - ignored except to note it */

\#[^\n]*            ; /* comment - ignored */

%%

/*
yywrap tells lex whether to stop at end of file or not. It is
assumed by lex that if yywrap returns 0 then lex can continue
looking for tokens. In our case, EOF means we're done with the
control file.
*/
yywrap() {return 1;}
```

# Index